THE DEVIL

CANTERBURY BOOKS

THE DEVIL

by

WALTER FARRELL, O.P.
BERNARD LEEMING, S.J.
and others

SHEED AND WARD — NEW YORK

SHEED AND WARD, INC.
840 BROADWAY
NEW YORK 3

Manufactured in the United States of America

CONTENTS

INTRODUCTION[1]

By Charles Moeller

SATAN is the father of lies and a murderer from the beginning. Falsity and violence—these two features are only too tragically typical of the present century. And of these two diabolical manifestations, it is arguable that falsity is the more essentially Satanic. We shall here attempt to show why this is so.

Contemporary man, confronted by the problem of Satan, is divided against himself by a twofold reaction, apparently self-contradictory. He is on the one hand fascinated by this mysterious personage, and on the other hand almost totally sceptical as to his existence and influence on the course of events. His morbid preoccupation with every species of the abnormal and the sensational, his insatiable need for ever more violent stimuli, his restless curiosity regarding the metaphysical and the occult—all these things are further degradations of an already superstitious religiosity. The devil, who is a past-master in the bizarre, cannot help but be a source of fascination; besides, he has staged a dazzling come-back in

[1] This introduction is based upon an article published in the diocesan review of Malines, *Collectanea Mechliniensia*, March 1949.

modern literature. At the same time, there is an almost total scepticism as to his actual existence: he is bundled away into the attic of discarded mythologies. Of course nobody believes any more in the pantomime demon king flashily got up in horns, red tongue and eyes of coal, rather as a confidence trickster in his working clothes; on the contrary, his trappings are in the latest fashion. But his influence has been watered down to a series of dangerous repressions within the personality. Cases of possession are accounted for on purely psychological grounds; the books of Janet—*De l'Angoisse à l'Extase,* for instance—are for many people the final explanation of diabolism in its entirety. The poet Valéry even goes so far as to make his Faust assure the devil that men no longer need his help in order to damn themselves. Let him who can fathom this paradox of the modern consciousness—that the majority of those who will read this book believe no longer in the devil.

What is the situation among Christians? We may speak frankly: whether among the laity, priests or religious, there is to be found a scepticism not far removed from negation. Though one may not question the actual existence of the devil—which would indeed be difficult, since it forms a part of revelation—one entirely fails to put into practice the conclusions to be drawn from it. "The devil exists, of course; but there is a happy medium between saying this and seeing his influence everywhere. We can leave all that side of it to the professional exorcists. For practical purposes—as far as we are concerned—men are only too adept at working out their own damnation."

No one disputes that genuine cases of possession should be left to the ministrations of those ordained by the Church to that purpose. And it is no less certain that we should be wary of detecting the devil's influence here, there and everywhere. But to leave matters thus and allow no place in the Christian world-picture for an exact theological assessment of Satan—this can scarcely be called logical. It remains true to say that there are a certain number of central theological problems which assume an entirely different aspect according to whether or no one takes seriously the existence and influence of the devil. Consider, for example, such a problem as the interpretation of history. The whole perspective will change inasmuch as one either gives full weight to the texts concerning anti-Christ and the final struggle of the Church against the devil, or, for all practical purposes, ignores them. Granted that it is perhaps a little hasty to say with certain theologians, however eminent: "Fundamentally, the problem of evil is the problem of the devil." For the metaphysical concept of evil viewed as a deficiency of being retains its validity; there is no need to dismiss the abstract aspects of the problem. But does this dispose of the problem of the devil? If, behind the world's evil, there lies a personality—if, in a sense which we must carefully define, evil is personified—it must be admitted that the point is an

9

important one; and this not only with reference to the non-temporal aspects of theology but also in its pastoral applications: what priest has not had experience of the devil in the conflict which he has undertaken to save this soul or that? There is scarcely a missionary who cannot further document the case with accounts which give one food for thought. There is something strange in the unavowed rationalism revealed by those who find something amusing in the words of St. Peter on the devil who as a roaring lion goeth about seeking whom he may devour.

THE DEVIL HIMSELF

By WALTER FARRELL, O.P.

LUCIFER, the bearer of light become the prince of darkness, has earned his name of Satan, "the adversary". He is the enemy of God, of man, of all that is good. It is no part of wisdom to underestimate an enemy. It is stupidity to cultivate an ignorance of the enemy to the point of blindness to his existence; for in such blindness it is impossible to face an enemy, let alone hold him at bay or conquer him. This is to invite defeat, to welcome slavery, to yield supinely to a conquest that in this case is radical, irrevocable, eternal.

Under pain of such fatal underestimation of the devil, we must know something of his angelic splendour, of the intensity of his malice, and of the agony of his punishment. Yet it will be difficult to see any of these things unless the splendour of Satan is seen silhouetted against the sun of the perfection of God, and in constant contrast with the limited capacities of man. In this light, one can see something of the angelic splendour (dwarfed though it is by the infinitude of divinity), and nearly all of the hatred, destructiveness and wickedness which feeds on despair. In a world that is uncertain of God and ignorant of

11

man, the Enemy of all that is good is perfectly disguised, safe from counter-attack; he is unknown. Men's terror of Satan throughout the ages has had solid basis in the devil's angelic powers and the malice of his will; that malignancy of the evil one is not shackled by ignorance, rather its full fury is unleashed on the world.

This chapter, then, is by way of a reconnaissance report on the Enemy who challenges so bitterly our every step towards perfection. What is he like, what are his resources, what are the foundations of his bitter opposition, what is his morale, what are the chances of his collapse before our defence or our attack?

It is of faith that Satan is a fallen angel.[1] That definitive description contains all the essential truth about him; fully analysed, it tells nearly the whole of the frightening story of the Enemy. As an angel, Satan is pure spirit, much closer to God than man.[2] The spiritual is not something foreign to us. We see it breaking through the material veil of men's bodies, its lustre making the difference between a vibrantly

---

[1] Fourth Lateran Council (cap. 1, "Firmiter"): ". . . qui [Deus] sua omnipotenti virtute simul ab initio temporis utramque de nihilo condidit creaturam, spiritualem et corporalem, angelicam videlicet et mundanam: ac deinde humanam, quasi communem ex spiritu et corpore constitutam. Diabolus enim et alii daemones a Deo quidem natura creati sunt boni, sed ipsi per se facti sunt mali" (Denzinger, *Enchiridion Symbolorum*, n. 428).

[2] This is abundantly clear from Holy Scripture narrating angelic actions which demand this inference as to their nature, and explicitly describing angels as spiritual, intellectual substances superior to man. Cf. E. Hugon, *Tractatus Dogmatici*, vol. i, pp. 572–4.

living man and an inert mass of decaying flesh. By his spiritual soul a man lives, breathes, reaches out to horizons that far outstrip the world of the animals; by it he is established as completely different from every other creature. Here, in Satan, there is no veil to hide the splendour of the spiritual, to limit or threaten its life-giving power, to cut down its horizons; here is a life-principle unfettered, a pure form flowing out into activity without hindrance or dependence. God Himself is a pure spirit, but the uncreated pure Spirit of limitless perfection; all that we know in this world, indeed all there is of life, of beauty, of goodness, are imaged shatterings of that majestic perfection. Of all these created fragments, the angel is the most sublime, the most nearly complete replica of the inimitable Source of them all.[1]

Perhaps one of the most startling characteristics of the devil, to us who savour drops of time so thirstily, is his agelessness. It staggers us to see him as young now as when the world was born, with all the undiminished energy and dynamic vigour of full, young maturity. Yet the fact is plain enough: a spirit doesn't grow up any more than it grows down; there is no way in which an angel can age, no moment in which it does not possess the full strength of its angelic life. From the very first instant of his existence down through the whole length of eternity the devil lacks nothing of his angelic perfection. He has watched the world grow old and the generations of men and women pass in unending procession

[1] Cf. E. Hugon, *Tractatus Dogmatici*, vol. i, pp. 572–4.

from birth to death; when the last of that long file has passed and the sun has set for the last time, Satan will still be young.

By his angelic nature, the devil enjoys the independence distinctively characteristic of a pure spirit. For ourselves, we glory in the freedom that stands out in a physical world as brightly as a fire in the darkness of night; yet it is only in the inviolable choices of our will that we approach the angelic mastery. Satan's life is independent of food, air, sleep, or any other thing ministered by the world beneath him. In God there is independence in knowledge, which is omniscience, in power, which is omnipotence, and in life, which is eternal, self-sufficient being. In the angel's pure spirit that independence is complete relative to everything but God Himself: its life can come from no other but God, for a spirit is not born but created; in regard to the material universe, it is completely independent, the master, in no sense the subject or servant, and a master that has no need for even the humblest ministrations of the material.

Among the vivid consequences of this angelic independence of the devil is his immunity to injury, to pain, to sickness, to death; indeed, he is even immune to the human discomfort of being crowded! Like God, and unlike man, he has no body. There are in him, then, no parts to be dismembered, no possibilities of corruption and decay, no threat of a separation of parts that will result in death. He is incorruptible, immune to the vagaries, the pains, the limitations of the flesh, immortal. Only God, by His almighty power, could destroy Satan, recalling the borrowed existence by which the devil lives; and this God will not do.[1]

There are no geographical difficulties in the way of the devil's activity. Since all reality depends every instant on the divine support by which it exists, God is wherever there is reality, He is everywhere; for God is where He works. The devil, a created spirit, is in place in the same way: the angel is where it works.[2] Unless this particular task exhausts the power of the angel, several material places can be the focus of angelic operations and together make up one place for the angel; the fact that he is busy in New York is no hindrance to his bustling in Moscow. His movement from material place to material place is accomplished with no more effort, and in no more time than it takes to shift the mind from one subject to another. The speed of light is a snail's pace compared to the speed of angelic movement; nothing in the world can escape the devil by flight.[3]

An interesting difficulty presents itself here from

---

[1] The conclusions stated in this and the preceding paragraphs follow immediately from the purely spiritual nature of the angels. Their purely spiritual nature is made clear in Holy Scripture where they are called spirits (Eph. vi. 12), opposed to flesh and blood (Luke xxiv. 39), described as living a life and performing works impossible to a material being (Tob. xii. 19; Matt. xviii. 10). This interpretation is universal among the Greek Fathers from the fourth century on; among the Latins, Augustine would still consider the matter doubtful, a doubt that persisted as late as Peter Lombard.

[2] St. Thomas, *Summa Theologica*, par. la, q. 52.

[3] St. Thomas, ibid., par. la, q. 53.

the pages of Holy Scripture itself. Angels have no bodies, yet they have appeared to men in physical form, have talked with them, journeyed the roads with them fulfilling all the pleasant tasks of companionship. But after all, if they are independent of all save God, masters of all beneath them, the angels can assume, and have assumed, the appearance of bodies; but they have not, as the souls of men do, become the life principle of these assumed "bodies". They have not, in other words, denied or cast off the purely spiritual character of their natures.[1] These apparent bodies of the angels could not act vitally: even under the guise of a physical form, the angel could not eat, digest, see, or hear, generate children. These "bodies" were tools of the angels, not a living part of them. The angel's mastery over the physical world is not at all to be compared to God's sovereignty. The angels' is a ministerial mastery, not a creative one; they can put to use the powers and principles implanted in nature by God, they cannot call those powers or principles into being.[2]

We see the devil, then, because of his angelic nature as a pure spirit, ageless, independent, immaterial, a life principle complete in itself, a pure form integrally whole in itself. He is dependent on God and independent of all things else: mirroring the divine resplendence in all its purity, the created

[1] St. Thomas, *Summa Theologica*, q. 51. The fact of the assumption of bodies is stated again and again in Holy Scripture; the non-living character of these bodies seems clear from the archangel Raphael's words to Tobias (Tob. xii. 19).

[2] Ibid., q. 114, art. 4 et ad 2 um.

pure spirit reflecting the incandescent beauty of the uncreated pure spirit who is God.

The perfection of angelic nature, the angel's proximity to God and superiority to man, finds its full clear statement in the sublimity of angelic action. Ordinarily we think of angelic action in terms of what the angels have been known to do in the material world and to the men who inhabit it; for that, after all, is our world, the world we know at first hand. Thus, we recall the avenging angel striking down the first-born of Egypt, giving the devastating answer to a profanation of the temple, going before the armies of Israel to strike terror to the heart of the enemy; or the tales of magic rites and diabolic wonders that ooze out of the dark depths of the history of devil-worshippers. Actually, all this activity is no more than froth on the surface of an angel's life. As in the uncreated pure Spirit the eternally intense activity is immanent subsistent Knowing and Loving which makes up the Trinity of the Godhead, so in the created pure spirits the unceasing dynamism of life is an entirely immanent thing made up of knowing and willing whose intensity is undiminished by time, not delayed by the necessity of a multitude of vegetative and sensitive activities as in men: an intense activity that is a stranger to fatigue.[1]

---

[1] This is the more common doctrine which limits the faculties of the angels to two, namely, intellect and will; as against those who follow Suarez in arguing for a special spiritual faculty, distinct from intellect and will, by which the angels move bodies.

17

For ourselves, we gather the crumbs of truth like beggars trying to reassemble a loaf of bread from discarded fragments. Our minds wander the world sniffing like bloodhounds at the traces of First Truth which make up the world of things about us, often enough losing the trail or dashing off on false trails. We know God through His reflections in things; indeed, we come to a knowledge of our own soul only through observing the activity of that soul in our actions. What we know, all that we know naturally, comes to us from a scrutiny of things beneath us or around us. God's knowledge is immediate and utterly independent; knowing Himself, He knows all things, for He is the cause of them all. His knowledge is not from below nor from above, but from within Himself. The angel, mirroring that immediacy and independence, has its knowledge, all of it, from the first instant of its life; not from a scrutiny of other things, but directly from the source both of truth and of things. The angel's knowledge is by infused concepts, had entirely from above, from God Himself; in fact, the greater the perfection of the angel, the fewer, more universal, are the concepts by which it knows all natural things. In its knowledge of itself, the angel perfectly images the divine, for it knows itself not by reflection as we do, not by infused concepts as it knows all else, but by immediate presence of its spiritual self to its perfectly proportioned intellect.

The angel's knowledge is, then, perfect, for it comes from God. It is immediate, since there is no need to gather it bit by bit through a search of the world. The angel has no need of the delay and labour of study; there is in it no room for error; there is not even the possibility of the obscurity with which passion so often clouds our knowing. There is no need in the angel for the caution so essential to ourselves as we pick our precariously slippery way down from the heights of principle to the levels of conclusions, or for the labour that alone will bring us to the heights of principles from the level of observed facts; for an angel knows, not by reasoning, but intuitively, plunging the sharp point of its intellect into the heart of a principle by one swift stroke that lays bare every trace of truth contained in it.

In view of that faultless angelic knowledge, we would expect a roaring fire of love in the angels; for it is the mind that furnishes fuel for love's fire, though in us often enough we neglect to put the fuel on the fire. Even at its best our love is a disappointing thing and in the depths of our hearts we are bitterly aware of it. The ignorance that blinds us to evil opens the way for the disillusionment and death of love; the momentary enticement of some new, bright thing makes fickleness a perpetual threat. Our love finds the path for its footsteps more by faith's obscurity than by the light of vision; reasonably we go to love's surrender with hesitant steps, slowly, almost fearfully, afraid to give too much or too quickly yet remorseful that we can give so little. Not so the angels. Following that perfect knowledge of theirs, the angels' surrender to love is immediate, unwavering, utterly whole and completely irrevocable. The fire of an angel's love is not built up slowly; it has no stages of mere smouldering, nor agonising moments of dying embers; rather the angel is immediately a holocaust, a roaring conflagration, aflame with a love that will never lessen.[1]

All this is true of the very least of the angels. With no more than this before our eyes, we are like a man breathless at the majestic lines of a cathedral seen through a haze, for we have seen only the blurred outline of Satan's angelic magnificence. For a fuller appreciation of the radiant perfection of our Enemy, we must keep well in mind the serried ranks of graduated perfection that make up the hierarchy of angelic choirs.[2]

This is a stupendous truth consequent on the purely spiritual nature of the angels. If you were to walk down a street in Chicago or New York and every one you met were to give back a reflection of divinity as startlingly different as we see now between roses and elephants or worms and men, you would have achieved some little insight into the world of the angels. Multiply this by the millions of citizens in Chicago and New York and you would

[1] This exposition of the knowledge and love of the angels is the common teaching following St. Thomas, *Summa Theologica*, par. 1a, qq. 55, 58, 60.
[2] There have been no definitions of the Church relative to the number or nature of the angelic choirs. The names themselves are to be found in the Scriptures, their use and order is sanctioned by the liturgy, while tradition has solidly approved the angelic hierarchy. Cf. Hugon, op. cit., pp. 726 ff.

be walking through a world staggering in its variety, its beauty, its perfection; where the mind and heart would find no such breathing space as is offered by the sameness of men. There would be no need for sharp alertness and sympathy to catch the beauty of individual differences; rather the heart and mind would be reeling under these differences that would be pounding at us every moment and from every side.

The angels, as pure spirits, have no bodies. There is, then, no question of generation among the angels, of angelic families or relatives. Each stands apart as a direct creation of God; and, as a pure spirit, specifically complete as an individual. In plainer language, one angel possesses more perfections than the one immediately beneath him by a step higher than that which separates a man from a dog. Each angel is a pure form; any differentiation in that form means a differentiation in species. Among ourselves, there is no such specific differentiation; we are all members of the one human species, differing as individuals by physical, moral or intellectual perfections that still leave us substantially, specifically the same as all other men. If a difference could be introduced into the substance of the soul of man, which is the human form, then the result would not be a man but something substantially different from all members of the human species.[1]

This is true of the lowest choir of angels; that choir consists of multitudes of pure spirits, each pos-

---

[1] This is the common opinion of Thomists and many other scholastics. *Summa Theologica,* par. 1a, q. 50, art. 4.

sessing more perfections than the next, in that substantial way. This, however, is only the lowest rung of the angelic hierarchy. To complete that first hierarchy, it would be necessary to mount through the more numerous multitudes[1] of the Archangels, and go on to the even greater multitudes of the Principalities, each individual spirit, you understand, specifically more brilliant in perfection than the next. There would still be the second hierarchy consisting, in the ascending order, of Powers, Virtues, Dominations; and, towering above that, the third and supreme hierarchy of Thrones, Cherubim and Seraphim.[2] These last, the Seraphim, are, then, the most perfect creatures God has made, their very name indicating something of the burning ardour, the sharp brightness, and clear consuming flame of a love that matches the most perfect mirroring of divine knowledge in creation. Of this countless host of the Seraphim, each specifically, substantially higher in perfection than the next, Lucifer was the highest; the "morning star", the "bearer of light", holding his rightful place at the very peak of created perfection.[3]

It is almost beyond our powers of comparison to

[1] That the number of angels is exceedingly great can be seen from Holy Scripture (Job xxv. 3; Dan. vii. 10; Luke ii. 13–14; Apoc. v. 11). There have been numerous estimates by Fathers and Doctors, all of whom agree on the greatness of the numbers of the angels. St. Thomas thought that the angels incomparably exceeded in numbers all material substances (*Summa Theologica*, loc. cit., art. 3).

[2] See footnote on p. 20.

[3] The more common opinion, tracing back to Tertullian and Gregory the Great (*Summa Theologica*, loc. cit., q. 63, art. 7).

balance one against the other the highest of the
Seraphim with the lowest of the angels. Yet we must
do more than this, we must see in contrast the highest
of the Seraphim and our own feeble selves if we are
to see something of the battle in which we are en-
gaged. Satan was the highest of the Seraphim. He
lost his title to that name of love by his fall, but he
lost nothing of his natural supremacy of that multitude in the highest choir of the highest hierarchy of
the angels. Seeing beneath him all the rest of that
innumerable choir, and on down through the other
eight choirs flashing back at divinity the infinite
facets of its sublime mirroring, we see something of
the Enemy we face throughout our lives.

Even this breathless height of perfection does not
tell us from what heights Satan fell; it tells us only
the perfection he carried with him into darkness.
For a fuller appreciation of the venom of this
Enemy, we must remember that these natural heights
of perfection were only foothills of the perfection
which the generosity of God called into being for the
angels. Satan, like all the other angels, was created
in grace, i.e., from the first moment of life, he was
lifted to the supernatural plane.[1] His natural life
was divinely perfected by the participated divine life
which we call sanctifying grace; the wide horizons
of his angelic mind were opened to the horizons of

[1] It is of faith that sanctifying grace is necessary for salvation,
and any works efficacious for salvation. Second Council of
Orange, can. 5–7 (Denzinger, op. cit., nn. 178–80); Council of
Trent, sess. vi, can. 1, 2, 32 (Denzinger, op. cit., 809, 811, 812,
842). That such grace was given the angels at their creation is
the common theological opinion.

divinity by the supernatural habit of Faith, letting him see through the eyes of God; his will was divinized by a charity and hope that would enable him to love God in a divine fashion and to stretch forth in eager confidence of divine help to goals that are possible only to God. St. Thomas[1] maintains that these supernatural gifts, necessary to every intelligent creature who would come home to God, were given to the angels in exact proportion to their natural gifts; in other words, the highest of the angels was, then, given the greatest perfection of charity, of faith, of hope, the most abundant share in the divine life of grace. Here was the mountain top of perfection, natural and supernatural, from which Lucifer plunged to his eternal doom by an act of his own free will.

Something of the terrifying powers of our Enemy is apparent from his natural perfection. We must grasp something of the tragedy that saw the light of such faith extinguished, and utter blackness descend to hide for ever the secrets of God; that turned the flame of that charity into the ashes of hate; that closed for ever the gates of hope and opened the flood-gates of despair; for only then can we begin to suspect the consuming rancour that hurls those diabolic powers against all that is good, and with no surcease.

The dazzling quality of angelic perfection would seem to preclude the very thought of sin. Yet the

---

[1] *Summa Theologica*, par. 1a, q. 52, art. 6.

ennobling fact is that heaven is not only given; it is also earned. Lucifer was created in sanctifying grace to crown his natural perfection; he was, that is, fully equipped to win the prize of heaven, but he still had to win it.[1] Because he could win, he could also lose. Like our own, his freedom was reverently respected by the action of God; and, like ourselves, if he were to have heaven he would have to merit it by the goodness of a free act, by his own free choice. Because the gates of heaven were thrown open to his efforts it became possible for him to go to hell. In this supreme test, the devil did not win heaven but lost it; or rather, he freely and deliberately turned his back on it. He was the first; all others who joined his hordes, whether from among the angels or from among men, were volunteers, haunting the halls of hell only because they so chose.

Yet that tragic choice of Lucifer does seem to present serious difficulties. Lucifer's free choice could not have been deflected by any preceding ignorance or error either in his natural knowledge (which was perfect from the first instant) or in the supernatural knowledge he had by infused faith, a gift greater in him than in any other angel and a perfect gift since it came directly from God. In him there could have been no rush of passion such as blinds men to the path to happiness, for passion is a movement of sense appetite, a thing impossible to a purely spiritual creature. Moreover, his will could entertain no least desire for evil since there was no disorder

[1] *Summa Theologica*, par. 1a, q. 52, arts. 1–4.

in the will and no mistaken judgment of the intellect to mislead it. How, then, did Lucifer commit sin?

The difficulty mounts when we remember the intense degree of sanctifying grace by which Lucifer lived a supernatural life, the superb perfection of his infused faith, hope, and charity. Actually, the difficulty can seem insurmountable only if we forget the sovereign will that God has given to angels and men; if we forget that regardless of the stupidity of sin, regardless of the perfection of intellect and will, angel or man can be evil if he so chooses. The question, then, is not so much how could an angel, particularly the highest of the angels, commit sin; rather it is, in the name of our curiosity, what was the sin of the angels and what was the process of that sin's commission?

For ourselves, we know that there are seven avenues of invasion open to sin attacking the soul of a man, the avenues which we name when we list the seven capital sins. It is immediately obvious that we must strike five of those out of our consideration when we investigate the angelic sin. Only the purely spiritual sins of pride and envy were possibilities to creatures who had no bodies, who had no use for money, no susceptibility to injury, no tendency to fatigue. Since envy demands pride as an absolute prerequisite, it becomes clear that the sin of the angels would have to have been pride.

This conclusion is today the common theological opinion. Among the early Fathers, chiefly because of the assumed authority of the Book of Enoch, it was thought that perhaps the lower angels sinned by lust for the women of the world; yet even when restricted to lower angels, the opinion chafed, for it was obviously difficult to find a place for lust in a bodiless spirit. By the time of Origen the apocryphal character of the Book of Enoch was clear, and the flat conclusion to the impossibility of lust in the angels was explicitly stated.[1] Envy as the angelic sin has had its champions, and with an apparent reasonableness. Lucifer might have been envious of the future exaltation of human nature by its union to the Son of God in the Incarnation; or of the future exaltation of men to angelic, nay to divine heights by sanctifying grace and the promise of heaven. But there the possibilities are exhausted; and it still remains true that pride must precede envy. There was nothing else for Lucifer to be envious of. He was the highest of created beings, there was nothing above him but God Himself and he could not be envious of God; for, as St. Thomas says, only a fool can be envious of what is so far above him as to be impossible of attainment. Lucifer was no fool. When it is said that he desired to become like God this must not be understood in the sense of a desire to attain divine nature or to dethrone God; but rather to be, in his own order, as God is in the divine order. As we shall see, that comes down to a desire for self-sufficiency that is not possible to creatures.[2]

[1] Confer *Dictionnaire de Théologie Catholique*, vol. iv, " Démon d'après les Pères ", cols. 339–49.
[2] Scotus and Suarez disagree with St. Thomas on the precise nature of this sin of pride. To Scotus, the sin was not so much

On the score of pride, surely Lucifer had more reason than any other creature; and his example, plus their own spotless perfection, would give plausible reasons for pride to other angels. Still, that pride had to find its way into the angelic world with none of the preparatory work of ignorance, error or passion. How did it happen? If we take a sinful act in its most obvious sense of a disordered act, it is clear that the disorder is immediately introduced by a choice of something evil, that is, by embracing a thing, like incest or murder, which is disordered in its very nature. It is not less clear that such a thing could not be done by an angel; we might mistake such a thing as good, or as having so much good about it as to be worth preferring to the divine, or, quite simply, because of the disorder already present in our own desires from the sinful heritage Adam has left us. There was none of this in the angels. With our long familiarity with sin, it is not hard for us to see another possible source of sin's disorder: perhaps we do not choose evil in this particular sin, but we choose a good badly. Take, for example, the matter of human love. Certainly there can be no question of its inherent goodness; but suppose we choose it evilly, suppose a husband does literally adore his wife, give her the worship,

---

a desire for excellence as a disordered love of self pushed to the point of hatred of God: and hence should be called a kind of spiritual lust rather than pride. Suarez considered Satan's sin as properly one of pride, but would have it consist in a disordered desire for a hypostatic union between the Word of God and his own angelic nature.

28

service, and preference that belong to God alone, suppose in actual fact his love does not go beyond his wife to the God who made her and in whom alone the marital love can stand—is there any question of the evil of this idolatry? Yet the husband has not chosen evil; he has chosen good evilly.

It is in this way that St. Thomas[1] analyses the sin of Lucifer and his angelic followers. Caught by the undeniable beauty, perfection, goodness of his own angelic nature fully comprehended, Lucifer loved it; that was as it should be. But his love refused to budge a step beyond this, refused to look beyond the angelic perfection to its divine source; he insisted upon resting in that beauty to find there the fullness of happiness, to be sufficient unto himself. As is the way of pride, Lucifer isolated himself, even from God. The sin, then, is to be found in his wilful ignoring of the further order of his own perfection to divinity; ignorance in the sense of lack of consideration was in the sin, surely, but *in* not preceding it, a part and parcel of the free choice that sent the angelic hosts into hell. Lucifer's sin consisted in loving himself (as pride insists) to the exclusion of all else; and this with no excuse: without ignorance, without error, without passion, without previous disorder in his angelic will. His was a sin of pure malice.

Because of his exalted perfection an angel who sins falls far; because of the perfection of the angelic

[1] *Summa Theologica*, par. 1a, q. 63, art. 1 et ad 4 um.

29

will, the angel who falls, falls but once. His love, you will remember, is not the faltering, hesitant, fickle thing that ours is; his choice is final, his embrace eternal, nothing further enters into his consideration to bring about repentance. The instant that irrevocable choice of pride was made, Satan entered into his eternal punishment, stripped in an instant of the supernatural life of grace, of the light of faith, of the loving union of charity, of the horizons of hope; cast out into the exterior darkness, and for ever.[1]

The essential punishment of Satan, as for the damned of the human race, is called by theologians the pain of loss. This means that the damned have lost for all time the goal for which they were created, the end which would have brought them eternal happiness; that they have failed beyond recovery, that there is no tomorrow with any less of despairing emptiness than today has held. They have lost God. We can understand a little of this hopeless emptiness from the crashing impact that destroys the lives of men who have chosen false goals; we must look to the false goals, for only these are irrevocably lost while man yet lives. To a man who has made health the goal of his living, an incurable disease destroys life's meaning and he pleads for extinction; the greedy to whom money is God, plunge to their deaths

---

[1] Both Scotus and Suarez agree that none of the fallen angels repented ; but both are of the opinion, contrary to St. Thomas, that repentance was a possibility to them and the time was given for it. Both agree that during that interval Satan and his followers committed other sins.

after a market-crash; the pleasure-seekers cannot face old age, and so on. In the case of Satan, the loss was irrevocable, and it was a loss of the true end for which all his splendid gifts were created; moreover, he knows sharply and clearly that nothing else can ever bring happiness, that it was this for which he was made, for which he was equipped, it was this that gave all meaning to every moment of his existence. It is lost; hopelessly, eternally lost. His despair measures up to the perfect insight of his great intellect; darkness is necessarily the colour of his days, bitter, self-despising darkness that strikes out at all light yet despises itself in the very striking; for this was not the fault of any other but himself.

Paralleling the pain of loss which is the answer to sin's choice, there is the pain of sense proportioned to the disordered indulgence of self-will. That pain of sense is inflicted on the damned by the fire of hell.[1] It is, of course, utterly impossible to burn a pure spirit, or to inflict an injury upon a bodiless creature; yet so material a thing as real fire could be an instrument of divine justice even against the fallen angels, as so material a thing as water can be an instrument of divine mercy to the spiritual souls of men. In each case the instrument is acting above itself to pro-

---

[1] *Summa Theologica*, par. 1a, q. 64, arts. 1–3. It is of faith that punishment of the demons is eternal, that they are excluded from the vision of God and that they are tormented by fire. Cf. Fourth Lateran Council (Denzinger, op. cit., n. 429); Constitution "Benedictus Deus" of Benedict XII (Denzinger, op. cit., n. 530–1); and Council of Florence (Denzinger, op. cit., n. 714). All of these characteristics of the punishment of hell are also clear from the Scriptures.

duce the effects of the divine agent using that instrument; but this is to say no more than that these things are indeed instruments, for that is exactly what happens with every instrument we ourselves make use of. St. Thomas[1] thought that the punishing effect of fire on Satan and his angels was one of confinement, that is, by the divine power this fire placed definite physical limits to the activity of the devil and his angels. That may seem a small thing until it is remembered that the angels are naturally masters of the physical world, supremely independent of all beneath them and superior in power to all the physical world can offer; and that the cause of their downfall was a pride that could not brook dominion even by God. Here, in the fire of hell, they are subjected to the meanest scale of physical being, subjected to a humiliation divinely proportioned to the exaggeration of their pride.

There you have Satan in his kingdom: engulfed by the blackest despair, bitterly hating himself for his plight and all else that escapes that same plight, yet hating himself yet more for this burning opposition to all that is good; beyond mercy and beyond asking for it; still consumed with the pride that hurled him here and subjected to humiliation beyond all bearing by the confining walls of hell's fire. With him in his rebellion against dependence on God were angels from every choir of the heavenly hierarchy;[2] moved by his example and entranced by their

---

[1] *Summa Theologica*, supplementum, q. 72, art. 3.
[2] This is the very nearly universal doctrine of theologians.

own perfection they followed Satan in his pride and now make up the élite of hell's company.

What is the social life of the demons' community? The answer to this question gives us the final, awful insight into the agony of Satan's punishment and the gnashing hatred that makes any good thing or thought an impossibility to him.

The sin of pride destroyed nothing of the natural perfections of the fallen angels, with the result that there is a kind of hierarchy in hell. There are two ghastly notes about that hierarchy: first there is nothing of peace about it but rather the violence of superior power that is at the same time galling to pride and merciless to inferiors; second, that supremacy is always a supremacy in evil and so a still greater source of disorder and the misery of disorder's realisation. Satan, as the prince of darkness, is more bitterly punished by the very fact of his supremacy in evil, as, in the physical order, a man is not made happier or more perfect by having a worse disease than his fellow sufferers.[1]

Pride is a complete barrier to social life, to common effort and common goals; for pride holds all else in contempt in defence of one's own excellence. It insists on being alone and being blind. So, the only bond of union in this diabolic community is the embrace of evil and the detestation of good. It is hard for us to appreciate the full vileness of this for, of course, we never meet any such unadulterated evil in this world. There is something of a parallel

[1] *Summa Theologica.* par. 1a, q. 109, art. 2 et ad 3 um.

in the impossible supposition of a group of men bound together only by the foulness of their common disease; not, you understand, by their common suffering and a merciful appreciation of the misery of the other, but by the one factor of foulness. Obviously, this would be no community at all, for the very foulness would repel any intimacy; and this is literally true of hell; it is not so much a community as a horde of the damned. It is not only that evil is no bond of union but a barrier to all intimacy; there is the even more intrinsic impossibility imposed by pride. Each of these demons is in hell because of the sin of pride; and pride, of its very nature, is self-love to the exclusion of all others, an imprisoning, isolating thing that is completely successful social suicide.[1]

In hell, with its violent subjection devoid of peace and its double barriers of evil and pride, it would be foolish to expect much of social communication; but it is hard for us to conceive the degree of communication's perversion that adds to the chaos of hell. In heaven, there is the constant sharing of truth by the superior angels to the inferior ones; and the constant speech which opens up the rich personalities of the inferior angels to the superior ones; but all this is the overflow of goodness and happiness, of treasure too great to be dammed up in any one creature. In hell Satan refuses to share his superior knowledge; hatred, bitterness, despair, detestation of all others combine to urge him on to any distortion of truth open to him, and away from any

[1] *Summa Theologica,* par. 1a, q. 109, art. 2 et ad 2 um.

least trace of justice. He is indeed the father of lies. As for the personalities of speech, it is unthinkable to one consumed by pride to open the doors of his heart to any of these others whom he so detests, or to reveal to another the horrors of guilt and despair that flood the depths of his being.[1]

We have begun to suspect something of the utter misery of individual life and the total destruction of social life where men are fed on a diet of lies instead of being nourished on truth, where the driving force at work is hatred instead of love, and where accomplishment is denied to the individual or held in theory and practice to a level beneath his powers. Yet, in the very worst of these circumstances, the lies must wear the guise of truth, love cannot be totally excluded, and there is heaven ahead for the most hopeless prisoner. In hell, truth, love, accomplishment have no place; there the lie holds full sway, hatred is in full command, complete and rampant injustice makes every individual a relentless enemy of all, and despair is the air everyone breathes. For a mind made for truth, a will made for goodness, and an existence that has looked to far, full goals there is no more complete, abysmal failure; and so no more devastating punishment.

It is true that within the merciful limits of divine permission the devils do tempt men, serving as exercise boys to the practice of virtue or executioners of divine justice.[2] It is also true that their conquests

[1] *Summa Theologica,* par. 1a, art. 3.
[2] Ibid., q. 114, art. 1 et ad 1 um.

of men or rather men's surrender to their blandishments can add human souls of men to the diabolic company. But this is by no means a kind of antidote for diabolic misery, a relief from unalloyed agony, or a release from the double pain of hell. There is no joy in hell's conquests, but only greater disgust, greater self-detestation, greater despair. The drunkard or the libertine can assure us at first hand that victory in evil does not diminish the evil but increases it, and the shackles of slavery to sin are not loosened by sin's accomplishment, but made more heavily secure. The malignant power and ruthless hatred of Satan are seen most clearly perhaps in just those terms: he has been more victorious in evil than any other creature, he has steadily maintained the most execrable accomplishment of sin. He is the Enemy of God, of man, of all that is good because he has been the greatest enemy of himself; no one knows that better than the devil himself.

THE ADVERSARY

By Bernard Leeming, S.J.

R EVELATION warns us that there is a disembodied intelligence which is malignant and ceaselessly hostile to men. If one asks whether this disembodied intelligence is a person—is there a *personal* devil?—the answer must be, that according to general Christian teaching the devil is not a person in the same sense as the Holy Ghost is a Person, nor in the same sense as you or I are individual persons; but he has real personality, in some sense comparable to divine and to human personality, but by no means the same as either. The Fathers of the Church often speak of the devil very much as they speak of sin and of death; and in many passages in their writings one could use the words *sin* or *death* or *the devil* indifferently.[1] It is not so much that the devil is made a personification of the death-principle and the sin-principle, as that death and sin are rather made the embodiments, in the temporal order, of what the devil is in the spiritual, and provide the aptest imagery in which to picture the devil. The devil is certainly not a man with horns, hooves and

[1] Cf. for instance, St. Athanasius, *De Incarnatione Verbi*, ch. 25.

37

a tail. Nevertheless, Scripture constantly uses personal pronouns of the devil; and though one must beware of attributing to that malign purposive intelligence the qualities we generally associate with a human person, the devil, according to the Christian faith, in some true sense is personal. Lactantius calls the devils *spiritus tenues et incomprehensibiles,* thin and unseizable spirits, referring to their physical nature; but he might justly have meant that they must appear thin and incomprehensible to our minds.[1]

It cannot be repeated too often that the devils are spirits and that consequently we simply cannot imagine them. Pictures of demons, insofar as they represent beings ugly and hateful, may convey something of the truth; but we must be very careful not to allow the imaginative image to limit our thinking or our faith. A spirit has no body, and hence cannot be photographed or subjected to any experimental proof.[2] We know what is a spirit of hatred, or of cynicism, or of pessimism: it is intangible and impalpable, yet most real, like "morale" in an army or a nation. Each of the demons is a special kind of spirit of hatred, of cynicism and of pessimism, an intelligence and will which opposes charity and hope and faith in the goodness of God. "The devil" is the chief of such intelligences and wills.

Could we know of this hostile intelligence apart

[1] *Div. Inst.,* ch. 15.
[2] For an excellent simple exposition of the nature of spirit, see F. J. Sheed, *Are We Really Teaching Religion?*, London, 1953, pp. 36 ff.

from revelation, that is, abstracting from Scripture and the teaching of the Church? Evidence might be alleged from a variety of sources: the amount of evil in the world, the cross-grainedness of conflicting good purposes, the wickedness which seems sometimes more than human; then various phenomena associated with possessed persons, the practice of black magic, alleged pacts with evil spirits, the deleterious effects produced on those who dabble in certain forms of spiritism; the temptations to which the best of men are subject; and, lastly, the very wide agreement among so many different races of men. To estimate the value of these reasons would be long and tedious, and I incline to think that the difficulty of excluding unknown forces of nature, and the liability of the human mind to error, makes any definite conclusion somewhat hazardous.

In fact, Christians believe in the devil because it is revealed doctrine, which involves mysteries; and it is revealed not only in explicit statements of Holy Writ—innumerable texts can be cited—but in the whole of the Christian outlook relative to what is called by St. Paul "the mystery of iniquity" and its practical bearing on human conduct and human destiny. For the sake of convenience the following four headings may be made:

First: against all forms of dualism, Christianity denies that evil is as ultimate as good, that an evil principle is as necessary and eternal as God. Evil rose not from the nature of things, but from the free choice of a creature of God.

39

Second: against Pelagianism, Christianity denies that man's present state, as we know it by experience, is the only possible state in which man can exist. Man, by God's goodness, need not inevitably be destined to interior struggle, self-division, and to death; and so our concept of man must be derived from Adam and from Christ, both of whom were so constituted that inclinations to disloyalty to God could only arise from without and never from within themselves. It was through the devil that man sinned and spoiled the nature God had given him.

Third: the doctrine of the Redemption affirms that the Word of God took flesh in order to "destroy the works of the devil" (1 John iii. 8), "that, through death, he might destroy him who had the empire of death, that is to say, the devil" (Heb. ii. 14). Christian writers speculated much about the exact manner of this destruction; but about the fact there was never the slightest doubt.

Fourth: the doctrine of the need of grace affirms that without grace no man is capable of "overcoming the wiles of the devil and the concupiscence of the flesh" except by daily help from God.[1] This touches the practical matter of guidance in the spiritual life, and of Christian humility.

To deal more at length with each heading:

[1] *Indiculus Caelestini,* in the year 431; cf. Denzinger, *Enchiridion Symbolorum Definitionum et Declarationum de Rebus Fidei et Morum,* ed. 24, Herder, Barcelona, 1946, n. 132.

DUALISM AND THE CHRISTIAN CONTEMPT FOR SATAN

Why Christians Mock the Devil

Dualism took many forms, but in all its forms it tended to belittle human nature. Generally, matter was regarded as bad and spirit good; hence the union of matter and spirit in man was looked upon as, at best, a transitory expedient, from which the spirit must escape in order to live its own proper life. Very often also the devil was identified with the eternal spirit of evil. The Priscillianists of the sixth century held that the conception and formation of the human body was the work of the devil, condemned marriage, and had a horror of procreation in all its forms. They rejected the resurrection of the body. In practice, they either inculcated unreasonable asceticism, self-mutilation and even suicide; or encouraged fleshly indulgence, since, as the body was in any case evil, nothing that happened in it really affected the soul. The Priscillianists were only one instance of those endless varieties of dualistic tendency from the Docetists of the first century, the Manichees of the second, third, and fourth, down to the Albigensians of the twelfth and thirteenth, against which so much of Christian controversy raged, and so much of Christian doctrine was formulated.[1]

[1] For the Priscillianists, cf. Denzinger, op. cit., nn. 238, 241, 242; the Albigensians, Denzinger, op. cit., nn. 401, 402, 428. On Dualism and Gnosticism no one is more penetrating than M. C. D'Arcy, *The Mind and Heart of Love*, London, 1945, pp. 47–54.

Against them, the Christian position was that evil originated in the free choice of a created spirit, and that matter was not eternal nor made by the evil spirit, but was created by God; and against them the final Christian argument was always the Incarnation, which at once showed that flesh and blood were good since God made them His own, and that the evil spirit could be overcome by man.

In the Christian scheme, the enemy to be overcome was not matter, nor even principally the desires of the body, but the spiritual power of a malignant but finite spirit. To the Christian, the devil had sinned by trying to be equal to God; but to the Dualist the devil quite literally was like God, indeed, not only like God, but another kind of ultimate God, making darkness and disorder and hate and vileness and falsehood as eternal and as powerful as God. For this reason he is by Christians made a figure of contempt, and the faithful were taught to despise him. In St. Athanasius's *Life of St. Anthony*, which was written probably about 357, and became exceptionally popular and influential, we read the ancient saint's exhortation:

When the prince of demons appears like this, the crafty one, he tries to strike terror by speaking great things, as the Lord revealed to Job, "he counteth iron as straw, and brass as rotten wood, yea he counteth the sea as a pot of ointment, and the depth of the abyss as a captive and the abyss as a covered walk" [Job xli. 18 ff.]. And by the prophet, "I will grasp the whole world in my hand as a nest, and take it up as

42

eggs that have been left" [Isa. x. 14]. Such are their boasts and professions that they may deceive the godly. But not even then ought we, the faithful, to fear his appearance or give heed to his words. For he is a liar and speaketh of truth never a word. In spite of his big words and his enormous boldness, there is no doubt he was drawn with a hook by the Saviour, and as a beast of burden he had his nostrils bored through with stakes, and as a runaway he was dragged by the ring in his nose, and his tongue was tied with a cord [Job xl. 19 ff.]. And he was bound by the Lord as a sparrow, that we should mock at him.[1]

This tradition, especially when any form of dualism appeared dangerous, was manifest in the whole history of the Church; and our English mystery plays of the Middle Ages provide instances of it. In them the devil is a comic figure: comic because his bigness and struttings and threatenings are quite futile. Hence perhaps in Gothic architecture the devils are made grotesque; they appear under multitudinous shapes and forms of men and animals, distorted and terrifying in isolation,[2] but as subsidiary ornaments

[1] Athanasius, *Life of St. Anthony*, in Wace and Shaff, *Select Library of Nicene and Post-Nicene Fathers*, vol. 4, Parker & Co., Oxford, p. 202. Cf. also the translation with useful notes by Robert T. Meyer in the "Ancient Christian Writers" series, no. 10 (general editors Quasten and Plumpe, Longmans being the English publishers).

[2] The late Henri Bremond in his introduction to Jean Bremond's *Les Pères du desert*, (p. xxviii) says that the early Fathers did not picture the devils as monsters, such as became the fashion in the Middle Ages. But in this he is quite inaccurate, for in the *Life of St. Anthony* there is explicit mention of the devil appearing masquerading as a woman, as a black boy, and appearing like "horses, beasts and reptiles", cf. nn. 5, 6 and 39.

harmoniously contributing to the glory of God's building.

Satanic Envy of Mankind

But in the patristic writings against dualism, the devil is not only an instance proving the sovereign goodness of God, the fallibility of every created will, and the futility of opposition to God; he becomes a very proof of the dignity of man. Wearisome becomes the Fathers' insistence that the reason for the devil's antagonism to man is envy and jealousy. They admit that a spiritual being is, in itself, in a higher grade and kind of being; nevertheless, God so endowed man that he roused the envy of the fallen spirit; indeed, the very fall of that spirit is not implausibly explained as caused by envy of man rising from pride. Various reasons are suggested for this envy of man. St. Cyprian,[1] St. Gregory of Nyssa[2] and others suggest envy, because a corporal creature is made to the image of God; St. Basil,[3] because man is made like the angels; St. Maximus the Confessor and Anastasius Sinaita, because man has dominion over the earth and control of matter, which the devil wished to have as his exclusive prerogative;[4] St. Athanasius quotes St. Anthony, because the devil did not wish men to go up thither whence he had fallen.[5]

[1] *De Zelo et Livore*, ch. 3, n. 4; Migne, *Patres Latini*, 4, 640.
[2] *Oratio Cat.*, ch. 6; Migne, *Patres Graeci*, 44, 456.
[3] *Quod Deus non est Auctor Malorum*, 8–10; P. G. 31, 352–4.
[4] Maximus, *Capitula*, 4, n. 48; P. G. 90, 1325; Anastasius Sinaita, *Quaest. ad Thass.*, 31; P. G. 89, 568.
[5] Athanasius, *Life of St. Anthony*, n. 22, op. cit., p. 200. This is the earliest hint I have found of the view common in St.

St. Augustine says that in his day several—"non-nulli"—held that the first sin of the devil had been envy of man; and rejects the view on the ground that envy really rises from pride and not *vice versa*,[1] in which Cassian, and later St. Thomas, follow him.[2]

St. Irenaeus has an enigmatic phrase, that the devil found in man "the beginning and occasion of his apostasy";[3] and some theologians conjecture that the occasion of the devil's pride had something to do with a revelation of the Incarnation. Suarez cites John viii: "You seek to kill me . . . you are of your father the devil and the desires of your father you will do. He was a murderer from the beginning and he stood not in the truth", and argues that the pride of the devil led him to desire the hypostatic union for himself; a view rightly disproved by the argument St. Thomas had given long before, that no one can really wish to cease to be, which a desire for the hypostatic union would involve. Nevertheless, Scheeben and Boyer modify this view of Suarez by conjecturing that possibly the devil's pride led him to object to God's uniting Himself personally with human nature, which would have diminished his own glory as an angel.[4] This would indeed explain

---

Thomas's time that men were created to take the place of the fallen angels; which St. Thomas respectfully rejects as not revealed; cf. *Summa Theologica*, par. 1, q. 23, art. 7.

[1] *De Genesi ad Litteram*, ch. 11, n. 14.

[2] Cassian, *Coll.*, 9, 10; P. L. 49, 736; St. Thomas, *Summa Theologica*, par. 1, q. 63, art. 1.

[3] "Initium et materiam apostasiae habens hominem," *Contra Haereses*, 3, 23; P. G. 7, 965.

[4] Cf. Boyer, *De Deo Creante et Elevante*, ed. altera, 1933, p. 517.

the devil's envy of man, and is not contrary to St. Thomas's mind, since he holds that Adam before his sin had a revelation of the Incarnation, not in its reparative purpose, but as it was the crown of glory, and the angels may well have been granted some similar revelation.[1]

When the Jews were seeking to kill Christ (John viii. 40), Our Lord accused them of acting under the instigation of the devil, who "was a murderer from the beginning". Now St. John also says that the devil "sinned from the beginning" (1 John iii. 8). Perhaps in Our Lord's words about the devil's being a murderer from the beginning there is a compenetration of truths: the reference is to the death his malignancy brought upon Adam and Eve, and to the death of Abel, which is a figure of the death of Christ (cf. Matt. xxiii. 35; Heb. xii. 24), and also to his first sin, which set up the first separation from the living God, in whom alone creatures have true life. However that may be, it is manifest that the devil's mind was murderous, and hence hostile to man, from the beginning either of man, or of his own rejection of God.

Thus, against dualism, the Church reduced the devil to his proper status as a creature of God, defended the essential soundness of composite human nature, and asserted the superiority of man without sin to the evil spirit, who even envied man.

[1] *Summa Theologica*, par. 2–2, q. 2, art. 7.

PELAGIAN DISBELIEF IN THE DEVIL

The Emperor of Death

The essential error of Pelagianism was that it denied the need of redemption, and bound God within the limits of nature as we experience it. Death is not only natural, but inevitable; sin is merely the decision of a will balanced in perfect equilibrium: the devil gave bad example, and, in fact, has small power over man, since man, if he wishes to use his free will, can avoid all sins. Grace is a mere extrinsic help, the giving of the law, the giving of an inspiring example by Christ; original sin is simply bad social environment, leaving man's nature and his capacity for good quite intact; the Church and a sacramental system are helpful for instruction but give no interior impulse to man's mind and will. Julian of Eclanum argued bitterly against Augustine, that to say that man is in any way under the domination of the evil spirit was unworthy of God and of man alike; and accused Augustine of Manichaeism because he held the inherited weakness of humanity. In Julian's view, all that is needed is to change the outward framework of man's life, to urge man to use his own free will, and humanity can save itself.[1] In this scheme, there is no need of a divine Redeemer; and, as Bishop Gore neatly remarked:

[1] Perhaps the best exposition of Pelagianism is by Anthony Cassini, in the appendix to vol. 4 of Petavius's well-known work on patristic theology. Julian's arguments are found in St. Augustine's *Opus Imperfectum Contra Julianum*, Migne, P. L. 45.

"The Nestorian Christ is the fitting Saviour of the Pelagian man."

Now if one takes Pelagianism upon the purely natural ground, it is superficial. It does not account at all for the empirical prevalence of evil and of human failure as manifest in history. It does not account for individual and social heredity and its influence upon man: on Pelagian principles, each man is born undetermined by his heredity. It does not account for the sense that all men have in general, and the saints more particularly, of the sad divergence between their ideal and their actual accomplishment. Lastly, it does not account at all for the inexpressible quality of grief on the death of loved ones, nor for those yearnings after a better life here, and for complete immortality, which are manifest in the hearts of men; and it reduced God to the status of a remote Law-giver.

Whatever, however, be the philosophic objections to Pelagianism, it was clearly not the traditional Christian faith. According to that faith, the world and man as we experience them are not the world and man as God made them, or as God intended them to be; if one looks at man historically, one will not conceive a right idea of the human nature which God made, but only an idea of the human nature which has been flawed and warped by evil. The only idea of man as God means him to be is to be found in Christ, and in Adam, the two really typical men who embody God's idea of man: and it is only by reference to them that man is to be judged, just as it is by mysterious unity with them that man fulfils his destiny. The sin-principle, the death-principle, both of which symbolize the spirit of evil, as they in turn are symbolized by him, entered from without into God's making of man, and marred the work which God had made; man lives in "the empire of death" and none save the divine Saviour can destroy him who has the empire of death, "that is to say, the devil" (Heb. ii. 14).

It is common among Christian writers to speak of man as the captive of the devil, or even as under the dominion of the devil; the Council of Trent speaks so: man through sin incurred death, "and with death, captivity under his power who thereafter held the kingship of death, that is, the devil".[1] Now, as to the exact nature and quality of this servitude to the devil, the Church has issued no formal definition; but it may safely be said that in the concrete it consists in man's inability to keep God's law and to avoid sin; without being joined to Christ through grace, man in fact will inevitably be joined to the devil, for, as St. John says, "he that committeth sin, is of the devil; for the devil sinneth from the beginning. For this purpose the Son of God appeared, that he might destroy the works of the devil" (1 John iii. 8).

Now this inevitability of sin lies in man's present nature. The Greek Fathers spoke of it as $\varphi\theta\delta\varrho\alpha$, a corruption, a principle of dissolution, in man,[2] a corruption which was at once physical and moral,

[1] Sess. 5, can. 1 ; Denzinger, op. cit., n. 788.
[2] Cf. St. Athanasius, *De Incarnatione Verbi*, ch. 6.

a general tendency to split up and divide all the forces of man, both in himself, and with regard to God and to his fellow men. Wars and strifes are a result of this corruption, and all the sins enumerated by St. Paul in his first chapter to the Romans.[1] The Latins called it "concupiscentia", drawing upon St. Paul's seventh chapter to the Romans, and meant that surge of passion, by no means necessarily of a sensual kind, though perhaps most obvious in sensual temptations, which makes man divided in himself, finding "a law in my members, fighting against the law of my mind and captivating me in the law of sin that is in my members" (Rom. vii. 23); or, as Mgr. Knox translates: "I observe another disposition in my lower self, which raises war against the disposition of my conscience, and so I am handed over as a captive to that disposition towards sin which my lower self contains." The lower self has more than a sneaking weakness for the devil, and in this sense man is captive of the devil; Christ, and Christ alone, rescues us "from the power of darkness and transfers us to the kingdom of [God's] beloved son" (Col. i. 13).

The Enemy Within the Citadel

The Pelagians, notably Bishop Julian of Eclanum, maintained that man by his very constitution as man was meant to die, and was meant to have the struggle between appetite and reason; and held that to speak of "concupiscence" as being of the devil was effect-

[1] Cf. St. Athanasius, *De Incarnatione Verbi*, chs. 4 and 5.

ively Manichaean, and implied that human generation was evil, in as much as it brought forth beings for the devil. No modern naturalistic philosopher could have argued more vehemently, or more acutely, than this heretical bishop of the fifth century; and no modern reporter could be more scrupulous than St. Augustine in giving the fullest exact rendering of the arguments and very words of the pleader. Those who look upon the Christian attitude towards sex as somehow morbid or unduly repressive can find argument after argument set forth in St. Augustine's painstaking enumeration of Julian's reasoning, together with his refutation of them, though Augustine never fears to let it be seen when Julian scores a point. Augustine's fundamental and almost wearisomely repeated argument is the need of redemption: if men are wholly good, if nature is completely uninjured, if self-control is within man's natural power, if infants are unaffected by their origin from sinful mankind, then what is the need for a Saviour, what need for rebirth in Christ, what need of grace, of baptism, of the Eucharist, of prayer? In particular, what is the need of baptism and what is the reality behind the exorcisms in the ceremonies of baptism? If the child is born in the state in which Adam was born, what need has it of baptism? Is not Christ the Saviour of infants? St. Paul says that Christ died for all: is this really true? And is it true that all died in Christ's death? And if all died with Christ, then, as St. Paul says, "being alive no longer means living with our own life, but with his life who

51

died for us and has risen again". But, on Pelagian principles, what is the sense of speaking of a new life in Christ? Presumably our old life, being good, would be good enough.

From this universal need of redemption, Augustine draws the inevitable conclusion that "all who are born with sin, by God's judgment, are under the devil, unless they are reborn in Christ";[1] and "we assuredly say the reason why those who are born are under the devil until they are reborn, is the contagion of sin from their origin".[2] Is this a Manichaean view, as Julian so often asserted? Augustine answers that, on the contrary, Julian's view is Manichaean, since he holds that the amount of evil in the world arises purely from the nature of things, and would have existed even in Paradise. On Augustine's teaching, evil is an intrusion into a better plan made by God; something which arose from the refusal of created wills to co-operate with their Creator. Evil rose first in the overweening pride of a created spirit, and then in man's weakened will, which the devil exploits; evil need not have been, and consequently *need not be,* since Christ gives power to overcome the rebellious forces within the citadel of man's soul. Augustine's doctrine of concupiscence as a sickness in the heart of man must be taken together with his correlative doctrine of the healing power of the grace of Christ. Evil desire, sin, death, all these bind men

[1] *De Nuptiis et Concupiscentia,* lib. 2, cap. 12, n. 25; Migne, P. L. 44, 451.
[2] *Contra Julianum Pelagianum,* lib. 3, cap. 5, n. 12; Migne, P. L. 44, 708.

52

to the devil, since they are the realm of the spirit hostile to God; but He who originally "made man right" (Eccles. vii. 30) "will form this humbled body of ours anew, moulding it into the image of his glorified body" (Phil. iii. 21).[1]

This "corruption" in man's nature, or "concupiscentia", must be referred back to God's original making of man, when his mind was subject to God, the lower powers of his soul to the rational mind, and his body to his soul.[2] The breaking of this harmony, this integrity, by the first sin, left man divided in himself, and left openings for the devil's entrance into the dark and mysterious spheres of psychological conflict; before sin, the devil's suggestions were only from the exterior, afterwards they can enter into the mind itself, since the mind is no longer completely whole and properly ordered in its relations to God and within itself.[3] Similarly, the temptation of Christ could only be by exterior suggestion, not by any interior influence upon Christ's imagination; for the latter presupposes some sinfulness, that is, some flaw in the integrity of the man, which could not be in Christ.[4] However, discussion

---

[1] On Augustine's doctrine of original sin and its effects, the two works in English which are best known are J. B. Mozley, *The Augustinian Doctrine of Predestination*, and N. P. Williams, *The Ideas of the Fall and of Original Sin*. It may be doubted if they correctly represent St. Augustine; and of more recent days they have been sharply criticised, as have so many of the "liberal" theologians, by the neo-Lutheran school, notably by Reinold Niebuhr in his *The Nature and Destiny of Man*.

[2] St. Thomas, *Summa Theologica*, 2–2, q. 164, art. 2.

[3] St. Thomas, ibid., q. 165, art. 2, ad 2.

[4] St. Thomas, ibid., q. 41, art. 1, ad 3.

of the nature of diabolical temptations must be reserved for the fourth heading.

THE DOCTRINE OF THE REDEMPTION AND THE DEVIL

Christ's Victory Through Defeat

In Genesis the absolute opposition between Christ and the devil, and Christ's triumph, is foretold: "I will put enmities between thee and the woman, and thy seed and her seed: she shall crush thy head, and thou shalt lie in wait for her heel" (Gen. iii. 15). The reference is to Christ and to His Mother, although this does not exclude a reference to the whole of the human race, since Christ is the representative man, the Son of Man.[1] The opposition is manifest at the beginning of Christ's public life, when the man possessed by an unclean spirit cried out: "Why dost thou meddle with us, Jesus of Nazareth? Hast thou come to make an end of us?"[2] In the parable of the tares sown in the field, the tares are the "sons of the wicked one", and "the enemy who sowed them is the devil" (Matt. xiii. 39); while in the parable of the sower "the devil comes and takes away the word from their hearts, so that they cannot find faith and be saved" (Luke viii. 12). The opposi-

[1] Cf. Pius IX, in his Bull on the Immaculate Conception, *Acta Pii IX*, t. 1, 607.

[2] Mark i. 24; and cf. Mark iii. 11; v. 1–20; vii. 25; Luke iv. 33; Matthew viii. 28; ix. 32; xvi. 21. It may be remarked in passing that possession in some sense by an evil or unclean spirit by no means excludes a natural disease, but rather affirms it; the devil being a spirit of disorder, his influence more or less direct is to be found wherever there is disorder, and particularly in the mental and spiritual fields.

tion of the Jews to Christ was inspired by the devil, as Christ repeats more than once: "You belong to your father, that is, the devil, and are eager to gratify the appetites which are your father's. He, from the first, was a murderer; and as for truth, he has never taken his stand upon that; there is no truth in him. When he utters falsehood, he is only uttering what is natural to him; he is all false, and it was he who gave falsehood its birth" (John viii. 44). The Jews declared that He overcame devils by the power of the devil (John x. 20), and was Himself possessed by the devil.

The encompassing of His death Christ explicitly assigns to the devil. St. Luke puts it: "But now Satan found his way into the heart of Judas, who was also called Iscariot, one of the twelve" (Luke xxii. 3); and Christ says: "Have I not chosen all twelve of you? And one of you is a devil" (John vi. 71). And at the supper, "the devil had already put it into the heart of Judas, son of Simon, the Iscariot, to betray him", and, a little later, "the morsel once given, Satan entered into him; and Jesus said to him, Be quick on thy errand".[1] When chief priests and

---

[1] John xiii. 2, 27. It should be remarked that Judas' treachery was real and had disastrous effects upon Christ's efforts to convert the Jewish people; He knew the authorities dare not take Him by day, and hid Himself at night, thus showing that His prophetic knowledge of what in fact was to come by no means led Him to act so as to bring about fulfilment. Quite the contrary: He condemned Judas precisely because his betrayal was disastrous. It is an interesting question what would have happened if Judas had not betrayed Him; human conjecture is baffled, but that is no reason for imagining that Christ automatically acted for the purpose of fulfilling the prophecies, just

temple officers came to arrest Him, He said: "But this is your hour and the power of darkness" (Luke xxii. 53). His crucifixion was to mean that "sentence is now being passed on this world; now is the time when the prince of this world is to be cast out. Yes, if only I am lifted up from the earth, I will draw all men to myself. In saying this, he prophesied the death he was to die" (John xii. 31ff.). And again: "He who rules this world has had judgment passed upon him already" (John xvi. 12). "One is coming who has power over the world, but no hold over me" (John xiv. 30). Although these sayings are mysterious, still it is luminously clear that Christ regarded His death as instigated by the prince of this world, and that His death was to bring condemnation and judgment upon this prince, the devil.

St. John and St. Paul refer to the triumph of Christ over the devil, as to a thing well known: "For this purpose the Son of God appeared, that he might destroy the works of the devil" (1 John iii. 8). "Because the children are partakers of flesh and blood, he also himself in like manner hath been partaker of the same: that, through death, he might destroy him who had the empire of death, that is to say, the devil" (Heb. ii. 14). And in Colossians St. Paul speaks of the triumph of Christ over the powers of evil: "Christ . . . blotted out the handwriting that was against us, with its decrees; lifted it clean away,

---

as the fact of the prophecies themselves in no wise relieves Judas or the Jews of their dreadful responsibility for their free choice of evil.

56

nailing it to the cross, and despoiled the principalities and powers, and put them to open shame, and led them away in triumph through the cross."[1] St. John in his vision in the Apocalypse says in resounding words:

"The great dragon, serpent of the primal age, was flung down to earth; he whom we call the devil, or satan, the whole world's seducer, flung down to earth, and his angels with him. Then I heard a voice crying aloud in heaven, The time has come; now we are saved and made strong, our God reigns, and power belongs to Christ, his anointed; the accuser of our brethren is overthrown. Day and night he stood accusing them in God's presence; but because of the Lamb's blood and because of the truth to which they bore witness, they triumphed over him, holding their lives cheap till death overtook them. Rejoice over it, heaven, and all you that dwell in heaven" (Apoc. xii. 9–12).

In view of this clear teaching of Scripture, it is not surprising that the Church has always taken for granted that "Christ became man in order to free us from the yoke of the devil", as the Council of Sens put it in 1140 against Abelard. The Council of Trent, in the preface to the statement upon justification, says that any understanding of the doctrine of justification, that is, of grace, must set out from the acknowledgment that, because of the sin of

---

[1] Colossians ii. 14. The above translation is my own; the passage is most troublesome for translators, as a comparison of the Douay, Westminster, Knox, Authorised and Revised versions will show.

Adam, all men "were to such an extent slaves of sin, and under the power of the devil and death" (Rom. vi. 20), that neither the force of nature nor the Law of Moses could enable them to be freed therefrom; and this in spite of the fact that free will was not done away with, but only weakened in its forces and biased.[1]

A Ransom Paid to Satan?

The practical bearing of this doctrine is that Christ died for all (2 Cor. v. 15), and His death is the objective cause why all receive grace enough to resist both their own weakness and the temptations of the world and of the devil.[2] But, if theoretically one asks: "*How* did Christ free us from the power of the devil? What precise aspect or relation in Christ's death referred specifically to the devil, so as to overcome him and release men from his domination?" then the answer becomes disconcertingly difficult and troublesome. The Fathers of the Church picture the thing as a struggle between God and the devil for the souls of men; and in that struggle the devil's weapons are lying, deceit, hatred, calumny, instigation to violence and to murder. God's weapons are truth, justice, love, praise, meekness and humility; and God conquers in the struggle. In depicting the conflict, however, the Fathers and ecclesiastical

[1] Denzinger, op. cit., n. 793.
[2] This is effectively defined doctrine, since the condemnations of Jansenism by Innocent X in 1653, and by Alexander VIII in 1690; cf. Denzinger, op. cit., nn. 1092, 1096, 1294, 1295, 1296.

writers sometimes use language which has caused scandal to some who have taken it too literally; Origen, for instance, says: "We were sold to sin, He redeemed us with His own blood from him who had bought us. . . . We term ransom that money which is paid to the enemy to free the captives he holds. The human race was such a captive, having been vanquished in the conflict with sin, and taken prisoner by the devil. Christ became our ransom, that is, He delivered Himself to our enemies. He shed all His precious blood for which the devil thirsted."[1] The devil had bought us with a special kind of currency: "His coin, the coin which bears his image upon it, is murder, adultery, thieving, and in general all forms of sin. Such is the devil's money, of which his treasury is, alas, all too full. With this money he bought us and received a deed of ownership over us"—the "handwriting against us" of which St. Paul speaks in Colossians ii. 14, which Christ affixed to the cross. As a ransom price, the devil demanded the precious blood of Christ;[2] God gave him this price by allowing him to kill Christ. Nevertheless, the devil deceived himself; because Christ could not be held in the realm of death, and in rising from the dead, Christ broke the power of death and the gates of hell, and made us all partakers in His resurrection.[3]

Often the Fathers, v.g. St. Gregory of Nyssa,[4] St.

[1] *In Rom.* 3, 7; Migne, P. G. 14, 945.
[2] *In Matt.* 16, 8; Migne, P. G. 13, 1397.
[3] Ibid., col. 1116.
[4] *Oratio catechica magna,* 26; Migne, P. G. 26, 68.

Jerome,[1] Pacian of Barcelona,[2] St. Augustine,[3] and many others, speak of the "rights" of the devil over mankind, and picture the redemption in such terms that it appears as a kind of legal transaction in which God had to respect the devil's rights and pay him his just due before man could be rightly liberated. But the real thought, as has often been pointed out by Catholics and non-Catholics alike,[4] is that through sin man belongs naturally to the kingdom of death and of the devil; and that in freeing mankind from sin and death and the devil, God's plan was not to make violent irruptions into the natural consequences of things, but rather to accomplish the redemption with a wisdom which respects the natures He has created. St. Thomas faithfully sums up the basic thought of the Fathers, when he places among the reasons which made the death of Christ a suitable manner of redemption the following:

Liberation through the death of Christ redounds more to the dignity of man, so that, as man had been deceived and conquered by the devil, it should be a man who should conquer the devil, and as man had merited death, so it should be man who by dying overcame death.

[1] Ep. 72 ; Migne, P. L. 16, 1245.
[2] *Sermo de Baptismo*, 4 ; Migne, P. L. 13, 1092.
[3] *De Libero Arbitrio*, lib. 3, cap. 10, 29–31 ; Migne, P. L. 32, 1285 ff.
[4] Cf. v.g. Petavius, *De Verbo Incarnato*, lib. 2, cap. 5, 8–18 ; Thomassinus, *De Incarnatione Verbi Dei*, 1, 3, 1–19 ; and more recently Gustaf Aulén of Lund, in *Christus Victor*, trans. A. G. Hebert, London, S.P.C.K., 1931, p. 64, etc.

And to the objection about the devil's "rights", which he puts thus:

> He who violently and unjustly retains something, rightly is despoiled of it by power of a superior. But the devil had no right over man, whom he deceived by fraud and by a sort of violence kept in subjection. Therefore it would seem more suitable that Christ should have despoiled the devil by a mere exercise of power without enduring death,

he answers:

> Although the devil unjustly had seized upon man, nevertheless man because of sin had justly been left by God in servitude to the devil; and hence it was most suitable that by justice man should be freed from servitude to the devil, Christ making satisfaction in His passion. For it was most suitable "in order to overcome the pride of the devil, who is a traitor to justice and a lover of power, that Christ should overcome the devil and free man, not by the sheer power of the Deity, but also by the justice and humility of the Passion" as Augustine says in bk. 13 of the Trinity, ch. 13, 14 and 15.[1]

There undoubtedly, as unprejudiced reading will show, is the fundamental thought of the Fathers: God's providence in allowing man to be subject to the devil's wiles and assaults was fitting and proper; and the manner of the Redemption by Christ's death, which enables man to overcome them, was equally fitting and proper. The struggle between Christ and the devil is naturally depicted by popular preachers

[1] *Summa Theologica,* par. 3, q. 46. art. 3.

in vivid style, and with embellishments which are not meant to be taken literally. Thus the cross of Christ is often called a fish-hook upon which the devil was caught: in avidity to swallow up all men in death, he seized upon Christ, who in fact was deathless and broke the power of the demon to drag men to death. The breaking of the devil's power sometimes consists in Christ's entrance into Hades, smashing the doors and permitting all the prophets of old to escape; and sometimes the metaphor of the devil being a dragon is pursued to the extreme of saying that the cross of Christ pierced a large hole in the dragon's jaws, through which all Christians who are seized in death by the devil, and would be wholly swallowed, can escape.[1] Sometimes the devil's power is said to be broken because he had a right to draw all other men to death, but when he caused Christ to be killed, he exceeded his rights, and therefore was justly deprived of his power over other men. St. Augustine even suggests that the cross of Christ was a kind of mouse-trap in which the devil was caught, the bait being Christ's humility and obedience.

To pursue this aspect of the Redemption in its

---

[1] Cf. v.g. the many citations given by Rivière in his *The Doctrine of the Atonement,* vol. 2, pp. 111 ff. This book, although containing much invaluable matter, by no means speaks the last word on the Atonement. Rivière's other volumes on the devil and the Redemption are marred by an attention to Turmel unmerited save by the necessities of local controversies and conditions. Aulén's *Christus Victor* does better justice to the thought of the Fathers; but it, too, is marred by an excessive desire to fit everything into categories, the great danger of the attempt to discover one leading "motif" in wide historical sweeps.

historical development, and its theoretic implications, would take far longer than the limits of this paper permit. One thing might be added: the Fathers do not regard Christ as merely one individual Man, but as somehow embracing in His humanity the whole of mankind. There is a mysterious union of all men with God by the mere fact of the Incarnation; and a further and still more mysterious union of those in grace with Christ as a result of Christ's atonement. Hence, in the struggle with the demon, it is not Christ alone who struggles and overcomes, but, so to speak, human nature itself, which is somehow universalized in Christ. In Christ *the idea* of man becomes changed from an idea of a being necessarily subject to sinfulness and death, and so to the spirit of evil, to an idea of a Being sinless, deathless and essentially victor over the spirit of evil.

Dr. D. M. Baillie, in his stimulating book *God was in Christ*, well says: "When we contemplate the story of Jesus we are bound to speak of the suffering and victory as successive phases; and so does St. Paul: 'Christ being raised from the dead dieth no more; death no more hath dominion over him. For the death that he died, he died unto sin once; but the life that he liveth, he liveth unto God.' But the same chapter gives us Paul's mystical doctrine of the union of the believer with the dying and rising Christ; with the implication that in some sense the passion and the resurrection are not simple episodes in the past, but are, both together, a present reality, an eternal

conflict with evil which is also an eternal victory'
(pp. 199–200).

THE POWER OF THE DEVIL TO TEMPT US

That we are tempted not only by the world and
the flesh but also by the devil, is clear both from
Scripture, and from the common teaching of the
Fathers and of spiritual writers.[1] St. Paul puts what
has ever been the Christian outlook in a passage in
his letter to the Ephesians, superlatively translated
by Mgr. Knox:

"Draw your strength from the Lord, from that
mastery which his power supplies. You must wear
all the weapons in God's armoury, if you would find
strength to resist the cunning of the devil. It is not
against flesh and blood that we enter the lists; we
have to do with princedoms and powers, with those
who have the mastery of the world in these dark
days, with malign influences in an order higher than
ours. Take up all God's armour, then; so you will
be able to stand your ground when the evil time
comes, and be found still on your feet, when all the
task is over. Stand fast, your loins girt with truth,
the breastplate of justice fitted on, and your feet shod
in readiness to publish the gospel of peace. With all
this, take up the shield of faith, with which you will
be able to quench all the fire-tipped arrows of your
wicked enemy; make the helmet of salvation your

[1] A host of patristic references will be found in E. Mangenot
article, "Démon d'Après les Pères", *Dictionnaire de Théologie
Catholique,* vol. 4, 339–84.

own, and the sword of the spirit, God's word. Use every kind of prayer and supplication; pray at all times in the spirit; keep awake to that end with all perseverance; offer your supplication for all the saints" (vi. 10–18).

If one may say so, it is an ideological warfare which seems envisaged: and truth, justice, faith, the word of God, apostolic zeal are the Christian's weapons. St. Peter says much the same:

"Be sober and watch. Your adversary the devil goeth about like a roaring lion, seeking to devour; whom withstand ye, steadfast in the faith, knowing that the selfsame sufferings are being endured by your brethren throughout the world" (1 Pet. v. 8, 9, Westminster version).

Here the immediate reference appears to be to calumnies or persecutions against Christians, and not to interior temptations of individuals, though these are not excluded.[1] The devil tempts to anger (Eph. iv. 26), to impurity (1 Cor. vii. 5), to refusal to forgive (2 Cor. ii. 10, 11), to resistance to the truth (2 Tim. ii. 25, 26), to abandonment of the faith (1 Tim. iv. 1), to pride (1 Tim. vi. 6); riches can be a snare of the devil (1 Tim. vi. 9), and the devil can transform himself into an angel of light, the better to deceive and ensnare (2 Cor. xi. 14). In Matthew iv. 3 and 1 Thessalonians iii. 5 the devil is named "the Tempter", almost as designating his function.

[1] Cf. Holzmeister, *Commentarius in Epistolas SS. Petri et Iudae*, par. 1, Lethielleux, Paris, 1937, p. 404. The text was a favourite one of the Fathers, especially of St. John Chrysostom.

Indeed, Christian tradition considers subjection to temptation by the devil as much a part of present human nature as is death itself. This is the reason assigned by St. Gregory the Great, and cited by St. Thomas Aquinas, why Christ Himself was tempted: "It was not unworthy of our Redeemer to be willing to be tempted, He who came to be killed; for it was right that just as He came to overcome death by His death, so likewise He should conquer our .temptations by His temptations."[1] Here undoubtedly is latent the thought that Christ is the representative man; and St. Thomas approves St. Ambrose's reason, somewhat mystical, why Christ was tempted in the desert, namely, that Christ went into the desert "in mysterio", so that He might free Adam from the desert into which he was driven after his sin, by conquering the devil also "for me" or in me—*mihi vicisset*. Other reasons for Christ's temptation by the devil are given: to warn us all that no holiness exempts from temptation, to teach us how to conquer temptation, and to give us confidence in Christ's compassion since He Himself has been assailed.[2]

Why Does God Allow It?

And here the question naturally arises: "Why does God give power to the devil to tempt men?" This question is answered by St. John Chrysostom in his famous letter to his friend Stagirius, who was grievously tormented by diabolical temptations; and

[1] *Summa Theologica*, par. 3, q. 41, art. 1.
[2] Ibid., q. 41, art. 1 ad 2.

his answer comes to this: that if God were obliged to destroy all beings which occasioned evil, He would have to destroy practically everything: our eyes and mouth and hands and feet, all of which can lead us to sin; and even the heavens and the stars and the firmament, which also can be an occasion of sin. Now, effectively the devil is only an occasion of sin; because we can overcome all his wiles and snares, which in diverse ways are to man's benefit: they stimulate man to virtue, keep him vigilant, humble, united to God by prayer; and, lastly, they add to man's glory by enabling him to overcome an adversary superior in intelligence and power. And St. John Chrysostom ends by the very quotable remark: "God would never have allowed you to be deprived of so much comfort, nor His servants to be so shamefully afflicted, unless He had known it would redound magnificently to your advantage and glory. And thus what seems a sign of God's abandonment of you, is really a sign of His affection and care."[1]

St. Thomas gives what seems the ultimate reason why God permits the devil to tempt men; divine providence, he says, secures the good of inferior beings through superior beings. Now the angels hold a middle place between God and man, and hence it is fitting that they should help men to God. This can take place in two ways, either by direct help, such as the good angels give, or by stirring men to good by attacking them. This latter the wicked angels

[1] Migne, P. G. 47, 424–48.

are allowed to do, "this helping the good of men, *lest after their sin the wicked angels should be lost to the utility of the natural order."*[1] This reason, of course, presupposes the native tendency and will of the devil to envy mankind and to try to encompass their ruin; and God allows the natural order of things to take its course.[2] To abolish the influence of spiritual forces, both good and bad, in human life would be as violent and as capricious an interference with the normal effects of the causes God has created, as it would be to prevent the law of gravity operating when someone fell down the shaft of a lift. The influence of good and bad spirits upon us is as natural as is the influence of good and bad men[3]; the existence of evil, indeed, raises questions which ultimately we cannot answer, but granted that problem, the permission by God to the devil to tempt us raises no particular difficulty, though it may, perhaps, sharpen or intensify to certain minds the general problem.

The Demon's Psychological Influence

As to the *manner* of the devil's temptations, it is, of course, part of the faith that he can only do what God allows, as indeed is the case with wicked men. There is common agreement, too, that the devil does not know the secret thoughts and intentions of men, except in so far as they are disclosed by some movement of the brain or nervous system or body; and the reason is that Scripture and the Fathers take

---

[1] *Summa Theologica,* par. 1, q. 64, art. 4.
[2] Ibid., q. 114, art. 2.
[3] Ibid., pars. 2–2, q. 165, art. 1.

knowledge of men's hearts to be a sign of divinity: "The searcher of hearts and reins is God."[1] Indeed in an English court, with reference to undisclosed intentions, Lord Blackburn cited the quaint judgment of Brian, C. J., during the reign of Edward IV: "It is common learning that the thoughts of a man are not triable, for the devil has not knowledge of man's thoughts."[2]

Very generally it is held by theologians that the devil has power to exert influence upon the imagination, the nerves, glands and physical organism, but not directly upon the will. This is St. Thomas's view, and he is followed in it by Suarez and the majority of more recent theological writers,[3] although the reasons assigned are not always concordant, and depend upon theories more or less well-grounded about the exact nature of angelic power. The view has considerable patristic authority behind it, notably St. Cyprian, St. Athanasius and Cassian; the Fathers very frequently attribute to the devil visions, impressions, emotions, especially of depression, and weariness in well-doing. It must be observed that this view of the power of diabolic influence over men seems to imply that the influence will be unobservable by feeling, ordinary consciousness, and perhaps even

[1] Ps. vii. 10; and cf. Jer. xvii. 10; Apoc. ii. 23; and comments upon Matt. xii. 25; John ii. 25 and xiii. 11, where Christ's knowledge of men's secret thoughts and of the future are urged as proof of His divinity.
[2] Cited in Cheshire and Fifoot, *Cases on the Law of Contract*, Butterworth & Co., London, 1946, p. 322.
[3] Cf. Suarez, *De Angelis*, lib. 8, cap. 18, n. 8; Pesch, *Praelectiones Dogmaticae*, vol. 3, p. 278; Hugon, *Tractatus Dogmatici*, vol. 1, p. 740.

unobservable by reason unless enlightened by faith. We are not normally aware by feeling or natural reason of the working in us of God's grace; and indeed it is only by reflection and reason that we know our own spiritual soul. Hence, it is not surprising that the influence of the evil spirit can normally be known to us only by the principles of faith applied to deducing his action from the effects produced in our feelings, inclinations and convictions. Here we enter the field rightly left to spiritual directors, who follow the general norms accepted for the discernment of spirits.[1]

One last question with which to end. Does the devil find any satisfaction when he is successful in tempting us to sin? And if so, how is this consistent with the general doctrine that the devil is even now in hell? If, on the other hand, he finds no joy or satisfaction at a victory over us, why does he exert himself to tempt us? Here we are face to face with our inability to imagine a purely spiritual being, in whom there can be no joy or sorrow such as we experience; but only, in the devil, as St. Thomas puts it, the "recoil of the will against all that is, and against all that is not" (*renisus voluntatis ad id quod est vel non est*). Hence theologians more com-

[1] Aldous Huxley, in his *The Devils of Loudun*, (London, 1952), is eloquent in denouncing superstitious belief in devils. The evils of such superstition, manifest in sixteenth- and seventeenth-century witch-hunting, are obvious enough. But it may be a greater, though more subtle, superstition to believe that unaided human reason is capable of finding a remedy for all the evils in the universe. Racialism, for instance, in its multiform ramifications, is a threat to human happiness with which mere human wisdom seems unable to deal.

monly admit some kind of "fantastical satisfaction" —so St. Thomas—or wretched joy at the power he has to induce men to sin; which very satisfaction in evil, as St. Augustine thinks, is part of his punishment. But St. John Chrysostom says roundly that the devil is in a frenzy—a mania[1]—and to try to reduce to reason the madness of inveterate hate and envy is an impossible task.[2]

Revelation tells us that there are disembodied forces which are evil, which are powerful, and which are permitted by God to play their part in human destiny. The world is as it is and not as we might like it to be; it contains cobra snakes, cancer, atomic bombs, just as it contains ideological antagonisms, stupidity, greed, pride. It also contains the devil.

Faith assures us that there is a means of victory: trust in Christ and the power of His cross, with the hope and charity which they alone guarantee. But if we reject or neglect these sole means, the prospect is bleak: the reign of falsehood, hypocrisy, hatred, cruelty, proud despair, unreason, death and unending corruption.

[1] *Ad Stagirium a daemone vexatum,* Migne, P. G. 47, 425.
[2] Cf. the discussion of Suarez, op. cit., lib. 8, cap. 15 per totum.

DEMONIACS IN THE GOSPEL

By Mgr. F. M. Catherinet

A REMARKABLE episode in Christ's struggle against Satan—a struggle whose vast proportions we know—is set before us in the Synoptic Gospels: the deliverance of individuals possessed by the devil. We shall consider in turn (1) the facts, (2) the problems they raise, and (3) the principles proposed by theology for their solution.

I. THE FACTS

(1) A preliminary series of texts affirm, in a general way, that the possessed were restored to normal health by Jesus. These possessed are distinguished from the merely sick; but these first texts give us no detailed description either of the trouble afflicting the patients or of the means employed to free them from it.

Jesus "was preaching . . . in Galilee and casting out devils" (Mark i. 39).[1] Before the Sermon on the Mount "a very great multitude of people . . . [came] to hear him and to be healed of their diseases. And they that were troubled with unclean spirits were

---

[1] We follow the historical order as set out by the synopsis of Lagrange-Lavergne and here cite the texts as given in the Douay version.

cured" (Luke vi. 18); for "they presented to him all sick people that were taken with divers diseases and torments and such as were possessed by devils and lunatics and those that had the palsy: and he cured them" (Matt. iv. 24).

When the emissaries of John the Baptist came to ask Jesus whether He was really the Messiah, before replying, "he cured many of their diseases and hurts and evil spirits: and to many that were blind he gave sight" (Luke vii. 21).

During His public life Jesus was commonly accompanied by the Twelve, and by "certain women who had been healed of evil spirits and infirmities" among whom were "Mary who is called Magdalen, out of whom seven devils were gone forth" (Luke viii. 2; cf. Mark xvi. 9).

When Jesus sent the Twelve to preach the Kingdom of God in Galilee, He charged them to "heal the sick, raise the dead, cleanse the lepers, cast out devils" (Matt. x. 8), thus giving them "power and authority over all devils and to cure diseases" (Luke ix. 1; cf. Mark vi. 7). In the course of this or another such mission John "saw a certain man casting out devils in thy name" (i.e., in Jesus' name), and, taking offence at this, forbade him "because he followeth not with us". The Master disapproved of this rather narrow-minded zeal, but did not deny the fact of the expulsion of the devils: "Forbid him not; for there is no man that doth a miracle in my name and can soon speak ill of me" (Luke ix. 49 and Mark ix. 38).

The seventy-two disciples received a mission

similar to that of the Twelve, to preach the coming
of the Kingdom of God in Galilee and Judaea. They
"returned with joy, saying: Lord, the devils also are
subject to us in thy name". And He approved of
them, saying: "I saw Satan like lightning falling
from heaven. Behold, I have given you power to
tread upon serpents and scorpions and upon all the
power of the enemy: and nothing shall hurt you.
But yet rejoice not in this, that spirits are subject
unto you: but rejoice in this, that your names are
written in heaven" (Luke x. 17–20).

When the Pharisees let Him know of Herod's
threats, He replied: "Go and tell that fox: Behold
I cast out devils, and do cures today and tomorrow,
and the third day I am consummated" (Luke xiii. 32).

The power thus exercised by Jesus was to become
the prerogative of the apostles after His death. "And
these signs shall follow them that believe: in my
name they shall cast out devils. They shall speak
with new tongues . . . They shall lay their hands
upon the sick: and they shall recover" (Mark xvi.
17–18). And so indeed it came about, as is testified
in the Acts of the Apostles (viii. 7; xvi. 16–18; xix.
12–17).

Let us note before we go further that it is not
simply the evangelists who here speak of casting out
devils, but Jesus Himself who (1) claims the power
to cast them out and distinguishes it from that of
healing diseases, (2) appeals precisely to this power
to vindicate His Messiahship, and (3) hands it on
expressly to His disciples as having a special place

among the miracles they are to work in His name. We shall have occasion to return to these remarks.

Now let us turn to the more detailed descriptions of the expulsions of devils.

The first occasion on which Jesus met a demoniac is highly dramatic. It took place in the synagogue at Capharnaum, at the beginning of His public life. "And in the synagogue there was a man who had an unclean devil: and he cried out with a loud voice, saying: Let us alone. What have we to do with thee, Jesus of Nazareth? Art thou come to destroy us? I know thee who thou art, the Holy One of God. And Jesus rebuked him, saying: Hold thy peace and go out of him. And when the devil [having "torn" or convulsed him—Mark i. 26] had thrown him into the midst he went out of him, and hurt him not at all" (Luke iv. 33–5; cf. Mark i. 23–6).

Similar scenes are mentioned in the Gospel record of a day spent by the Saviour at Capharnaum. He healed the sick. "And devils went out from many, crying out and saying: Thou art the Son of God. And rebuking them he suffered them not to speak [and to say who he was] for they knew that he was Christ" (Luke iv. 41; cf. Mark i. 34; Matt. viii. 16). St. Mark, speaking of like happenings, tells us (iii. 11–12): "And the unclean spirits, when they saw him, fell down before him: and they cried, saying: Thou art the Son of God. And he strictly charged them that they should not make him known."

It was by action from a distance that the devil was cast out of the daughter of the Syrophenician woman.

The mother, a Gentile, came to Jesus and fell at His feet and besought Him, without allowing herself to be put off by two rebuffs; and Jesus said to her at last: "For this saying [that the whelps may eat of the fallen crumbs of the children] go thy way. The devil is gone out of thy daughter. And when she was come into her house she found the girl lying upon the bed and that the devil was gone out" (Mark vii. 25–30; cf. Matt. xv. 21–8).

In the case of the deformed woman cured in the synagogue on the sabbath, we must attend carefully both to the description of the infirmity and to its attribution to the devil by the evangelist, St. Luke, and by Jesus Himself.

And he was teaching in their synagogue on their sabbath. And behold there was a woman who had a spirit of infirmity eighteen years. And she was bowed together: neither could she look upward at all. Whom when Jesus saw, he called her unto him and said to her: Woman thou art delivered from thine infirmity. And he laid his hands upon her, and immediately she was made straight and glorified God. And the ruler of the synagogue (being angry that Jesus had healed on the sabbath), answering said . . . And the Lord answering him, said: Ye hypocrites, doth not every one of you, on the sabbath day, loose his ox or his ass from the manger and lead them to water? And ought not this daughter of Abraham, whom Satan hath bound, lo, these eighteen years, be loosed from this bond on the sabbath day?" (Luke xiii. 10–17).[1]

[1] Here, in this study of the Gospel narratives, and following the practically unanimous voice of the exegetes, we shall desig-

To this case of possession, whose effects, as described, are strikingly similar to the symptoms of a local paralysis, we must add two others in which the descriptive analysis is more picturesque and more complete. Both are reported by the three Synoptic Gospels, by St. Matthew with sobriety, by St. Luke with precision, and by St. Mark with a wealth of vivid detail that seems to come straight from life. We shall reproduce St. Mark's accounts, completing them here and there when necessary with the bracketed matter from the other evangelists.

---

nate as possessed all those subjects said by Jesus to have a devil; a devil producing a disturbance of health which ceases on his expulsion. The proof of this active presence of the devil lies in the word and attitude of the divine Master. The modern exorcist, guided by the Ritual, is deprived of this infallible support in judging the case submitted to him. He has to begin by establishing the presence and activity of the devil, by noting the preternatural phenomena which indicate this presence and this activity. He has to avail himself here of the "principle of economy", which very rightly demands that the diabolical explanation shall not be entertained if any natural explanation is adequate. But in the Gospel the question is settled already: the presence and action of the devil is a datum. Even in the case of the deformed woman, where it is not explicitly stated that the devil is *here and now present* in the patient, and from whom he is not, *in so many words,* cast out, he cause of the malady is nevertheless said by St. Luke to have been "a spirit of infirmity" who had afflicted her for eighteen years; and Jesus Himself goes on to say that the spirit's name was Satan, who had "bound her, lo, these eighteen years"— and "ought not this daughter of Abraham to be loosed from his bond on the sabbath day?" Père de Tonquédec is quite justified in remarking that for a present-day exorcist there is mere no case of a *possession* (in the modern and full sense of he term) that could be strictly *demonstrated* by the tests at his disposal; but in the Gospel, nevertheless, the malady is presented as due to the devil, and the cure as a rupture of a bond established and maintained by Satan. That is why the Gospel commentators commonly reckon it among the cases of "possession".

77

Here first is the case of the possessed of Gerasa.

Jesus lands on the eastern side of the lake of Genesareth, in the country of the Gerasenes.

And as he went out of the ship, immediately there met him out of the monuments a man with an unclean spirit, who had his dwelling in the tombs: and no man could bind him, not even with chains. For having been often bound with fetters and chains, he had burst the chains and broken the fetters in pieces: and no one could tame him. And he was always day and night in the monuments and in the mountains, crying and cutting himself with stones. [He had gone un-clothed for a long time—Luke.]

And seeing Jesus afar off, he ran and adored him. And crying with a loud voice he said: What have I to do with thee, Jesus the Son of the most high God? I adjure thee by God that thou torment me not. For he said unto him: Go out of the man, thou unclean spirit. And he asked him: What is thy name? And he saith unto him: My name is Legion, for we are many. And he besought him much, that he would not drive him away [into the Abyss—Luke] out of the country.

And there was there near the mountain a great herd of swine, feeding. And the spirits besought him, say-ing: Send us into the swine, that we may enter into them. And Jesus immediately gave them leave. And the unclean spirits going out, entered into the swine. And the herd with great violence was carried head-long into the sea, being about two thousand, and were stifled in the sea.

And they that fed them fled and told it in the city and in the fields. And they went out to see what was done. And they came to Jesus. And they see him that was troubled with the devil, sitting clothed, and well in his wits: and they were afraid. . . . And they began to pray him that he would depart from their coasts. And when he went up into the ship, he that had been troubled with the devil began to beseech him that he might be with him. And he admitted him not, but saith to him: Go into thy house to thy friends, and tell them how great things the Lord hath done for thee, and hath had mercy on thee.

And this he did not only in "the whole city" Luke), but "in Decapolis" (Mark v. 20).

Of all the Gospel narratives this is the one that gives us the clearest characterisation of the devils in possession of a human organism. There they create and maintain certain morbid disturbances not far removed from madness. They possess a penetrating intelligence, and know who Jesus is. They prostrate themselves before Him unblushingly, beseeching, adjuring Him by God not to send them back to the Abyss, but rather to allow them to go into the swine and take up their abode there. Hardly have they entered into the swine, than with a display of power not less surprising than their versatility, they bring about the cruel and wicked destruction of the poor beasts in which they had begged refuge. Craven, obsequious, powerful, malicious, versatile and even grotesque—all these traits, here strongly marked, reappear in varying degrees in the other Gospel narratives of the expulsion of devils.[1]

[1] The ridiculous, vulgar and malicious side of diabolical possessions appears also in the narratives of the Acts, notably in xix. 13–17, where at Ephesus we meet with "some also of the

79

The demoniac whom Jesus found at the foot of
the Mountain of the Transfiguration, and whose
malady baffled the apostles, displays, along with
deaf-mutism, all the clinical indications of epilepsy.
Here once more we shall have to turn to St. Mark's
account (ix. 13–28):

And coming to his disciples he saw a great multitude
about them and the scribes disputing with them. . . .
And he asked them: What do you question about
among you? And one of the multitude, answering,
said: Master, I have brought my son to thee, having
a dumb spirit. Who, wheresoever he taketh him,
dasheth him: and he foameth and gnasheth with the
teeth; and pineth away. And I spoke to thy disciples
to cast him out: and they could not. Who answering
them said: O incredulous generation, how long shall
I be with you? How long shall I suffer you? Bring
him unto me. And they brought him.

And when he had seen him, immediately the spirit
troubled him; and being thrown down upon the ground,
he rolled about foaming. And he asked his father:
How long time is it since this hath happened unto
him? But he said: From his infancy. And oftentimes
hath he cast him into the fire and into waters to
destroy him. But if thou canst do anything, help us,
having compassion on us. And Jesus saith to him: If

Jewish exorcists who went about [and] attempted to invoke
over them that had evil spirits the name of the Lord Jesus. . . .
And there were certain men, seven sons of Sceva, a Jew, a
chief priest, that did this". They had cause enough to rue it,
for one fine day one of those possessed replied: "Jesus I know:
and Paul I know. But who are you? And the man in whom
the wicked spirit was, leaping upon them and mastering them
both, prevailed against them, so that they fled out of that house
naked and wounded."

thou canst believe, all things are possible to him that believeth. And immediately the father of the boy crying out, with tears said: I do believe, Lord. Help my unbelief.

And when Jesus saw the multitude running together, he threatened the unclean spirit, saying to him: Deaf and dumb spirit, I command thee, go out of him, and enter not any more into him. And crying out and greatly tearing him, he went out of him. And he became as dead, so that many said: He is dead. But Jesus, taking him by the hand, lifted him up. And he arose. [And Jesus restored him to his father—Luke.]

And when he was come into the house, his disciples secretly asked him: Why could we not cast him out? And he said to them: This kind can go out by nothing but by prayer and fasting.

II. THE PROBLEMS

How find the correct interpretation of these data?

(1) Although the evangelists sometimes use the word "heal" or "cure" in connection with the deliverance of the possessed by Jesus,[1] the contexts themselves suggest that this "healing" has to be taken in a special sense. Thus the woman with the bent back is represented as "delivered from her infirmity" in Luke xiii. 12, after having been "bound by Satan these eighteen years", and now she is to be "loosed from this bond" (verse 16). So also the epileptic is "cured" but precisely because the "unclean spirit" has been "cast out" (Luke ix. and parallels). The fact is that the deliverance of possessed persons, in all cases where it is related in any

[1] Cf. Luke vii. 21; viii. 2; ix. 43, etc.

81

detail, is presented under conditions which clearly differentiate it from the cure of mere disease.

To be precise, the plight of the possessed is attributed to "the devil", a hidden, malicious being, capable of tempting even Jesus; a being who is "the power of darkness", and has "his hour" during the events of the Passion; who acts with as much deceit and wickedness as intelligence. He "enters" the possessed, he "dwells" there, and "còmes back"; he "enters" into the swine. The possessed "has a devil", an "unclean devil" (Luke iv. 33); he is an "unclean spirit" (Mark i. 23). The devil "goes out" of the possessed, and into another place, into the desert, into the swine, into the Abyss; and that precisely because he is "driven"—that is the word most commonly used. When Jesus approaches he shows "terror", he "falls down", "beseeches", declares that he "knows" the supernatural status of Jesus. The latter "speaks" to him, "questions" him, gives him "commands" and "permissions" and imposes silence. *Not one* of these traits can be found in the behaviour of the merely sick towards Jesus, nor in the way in which Jesus sets out to cure them.

(2) The attitude of Jesus in the presence of the possessed does not allow a Catholic, nor even any attentive historian, to think that in acting and speaking as He did He was merely accommodating Himself to the ignorances and prejudices of His contemporaries.

What is in question here is no mere current mode of speech (as when we describe the sun as "rising" from the horizon, and "going up" towards the zenith), but a doctrine that expresses an essential aspect of the mission of the God-man in this world: "For this purpose the Son of God appeared, that he might destroy the works of the devil" (1 John iii. 8). On points of such importance touching the supernatural world Jesus could by no means indulge in tolerant equivocations. He never used them. Look at the ninth chapter of the Gospel of St. John. There we have the case of the man born blind. The disciples, either personally mistaken or possibly sharing the views of the Essenes or some other Jewish sect, asked the Master: "Who has sinned, this man or his parents, that he should be born blind?" They were not alone in putting down his blindness to sin. When the man, now cured, was standing up bravely to the interrogation of the Sanhedrin, they cut him short with: "Thou wast wholly born in sins, and dost thou teach us?" Here, then, we are certainly in the presence of a prejudice or error common among the contemporaries of Jesus. But since this error touched the supernatural order Jesus allowed Himself no conformism; He would entertain nothing but the simple truth, and put it without compromise: "Neither hath this man sinned nor his parents; but that the works of God should be made manifest in him."

Now Jesus, who would not so much as once let pass a mistaken word dropped on matters of religion, *never* corrected His disciples' expressions on the subject of demoniac possessions. And He spoke of them Himself in identical terms, strictly squaring His action in the matter with the ideas and language of His countrymen. It is plain that He simply held them.

What is more, He took up a position of His own on the point and defended it. The controversy is set out in all three Synoptic Gospels (Luke xi. 14–26; Mark iii. 22–30; Matt. xii. 22–45). Jesus had cast out a devil who had made his victim blind and dumb. The Pharisees accused Him of driving out lesser devils by the power of Beelzebub, "Prince of the devils". The occasion was a good one to let them know that there was here no question of demoniac possession but only of disease. Jesus did not seize it. The devils, he said, do not cast each other out; if they did, they would long ago have put an end to their own "kingdom". . . . No, they are driven out because they have now come up against someone "stronger than themselves", and their defeat is the sign that "the kingdom of God is come upon you". This defeat will not prevent Satan from launching a counter-offensive, and it may even have a striking success in some cases, since the devil driven out will come back "with seven other spirits more wicked than himself". That is because human bad faith, such as had just been shown in the Pharisees' accusation of Jesus, constitutes that voluntary and obstinate blindness called "blasphemy against the Holy Ghost", and opens the way to the definitive return of the reinforced enemy. Here then, as elsewhere, and even more clearly than elsewhere, it is evident that

Jesus speaks of the devil and of possession by the devil as realities, and that on this point He finds no errors to dispel either among His disciples or His adversaries.

The true problem raised by these possessions does not lie there. We must now try to formulate it in precise terms and see whether this may suggest some line of thought on which its solution may be found.

(3) Let us abstract for the moment from the method that Jesus adopts in delivering the possessed and consider only the symptoms of their state as given in the more or less detailed descriptions preserved in the Gospels. It can hardly be doubted that a study of the morbid symptoms, and of these *alone*, would lead every doctor to see in the deformed woman a paralytic, in the energumen of Gerasa a furious madman, in the child healed on the morrow of the Transfiguration an epileptic—and so on. Moreover, each possession that is individually set before us is accompanied by an infirmity: the devil strikes his victim dumb (Matt. ix. 32; xii. 22; Mark ix. 16; Luke xi. 14); deaf and dumb (Mark vii. 32); dumb and blind (Matt. xii. 22); "lunatic" (Matt. xvii. 14); he provokes convulsive crises (Mark i. 26; Luke iv. 35; and especially Mark ix. 18–20 and parallels above cited). From a purely medical standpoint all these morbid phenomena are closely connected with a diseased state of the nervous system. We can readily appreciate how a psychiatrist might be tempted to isolate these phenomena, to base his whole judgment on nothing else, and to conclude

that under the name of "possession" the Gospels present us simply with cases of neurosis. Now at last we face the problem of demoniac possession in all its force.

(4) But to set out to solve this problem from a purely medical standpoint is to follow a false trail. Only a part of the facts could be thus explained. How do these neurotics recognise and proclaim the Messiah? How could their disorders be instantaneously transferred to a herd of swine and bring about its destruction? How comes it that the wonder-worker here acts by threats not directed against the patient himself, but against another? How is it that He always effects by one brief word a cure that is instantaneous, complete and final? Think of the time a modern psychiatrist needs, the slow and laborious methods of persuasion he employs, in order to "cure"—when he does cure—or even to ameliorate the disorders of his pitiable clientèle.

These questions become still more pressing when we remember that all the ills enumerated above—dumbness, deafness, blindness, paralysis, apparently due to the same neuropathic cause—are often met with in the Gospel unaccompanied by any mention of the devil, and are cured by means that have absolutely nothing in common with these imperious and threatening exorcisms, or with conversations with an interlocutor who is other than the patient. We must cite some examples of this.

Here is the case of the deaf-mute of Mark vii. 32–5 (the Greek text makes him a "deaf-stammerer" which still more clearly indicates the nervous character of the trouble).

> And taking him from the multitude apart, he put his fingers into his ears: and spitting, he touched his tongue. And looking up to heaven, he groaned and said to him: Ephpheta, which is, Be thou opened. And immediately his ears were opened, and the string of his tongue was loosed, and he spoke right.

No mention of the devil, no threats, only a few symbolical gestures with a word expressing their meaning. It is simply a miraculous cure of a nervous malady. It is not the expulsion of a devil.

Everybody remembers the cure from a distance of the paralysed servant of the centurion of Capharnaum who declared himself unworthy to receive Jesus under his roof (Matt. viii. 5–13; Luke vii. 1–10); also that of the paralytic whose zealous friends uncovered the roof of the house where Jesus was teaching, and let down the bed with the patient at Jesus' feet; and whom the Master cured with a word affirming that "the Son of Man hath power on earth to forgive sins" (Mark ii. 1–12 and parallels). Once more, no threats, no exorcisms, but words full of kindness for both centurion and paralytic, with no attribution of the illness to the malice of the devil.

And here is the cure of the blind man[1] as related by St. Mark (viii. 22–6):

[1] It is not certain whether this particular case of blindness can be put down to nervous causes: unlike the case of the deaf and blind demoniac (Matt. xii. 22) noted above. The comparison shows at least that blindness, whatever its immediate cause,

And they came to Bethsaida; and they bring to him a blind man, and they besought him that he would touch him. And taking the blind man by the hand, he led him out of the town : and spitting upon his eyes, laying his hands on him, he asked him if he saw anything. And looking up, he said : I see men as it were trees, walking. After that again he laid his hands upon his eyes and he began to see and was restored, so that he saw all things clearly. And he sent him into his house.

Here, if we do not mistake, is the sole case in the Gospels of a "progressive" miraculous cure, effected, however, in a few moments and without any of the long and complicated methods of modern psychiatry. But here again are no devils, no threats, no commands to "go out of him", and no exorcism.

It will be seen from these texts that the two notions of "nervous malady" and "diabolic possession" do not always coincide exactly. The Gospel presents possessions accompanied by neuroses, and neuroses pure and simple. The means used to restore the patients to their normal state also differ according to which of these two categories the subjects belong to. Any simple identification of possession with a nervous malady is incompatible with the Gospel. After all these explanations and détours we can now at last condense the enunciation of the real problem raised by these Gospel narratives into the following formula :

whether nervous or other, was sometimes taken by Jesus for a *disease* to be cured without exorcism, and sometimes for the result of *possession,* to be put an end to by expelling the devil.

88

Whence comes it that diabolical possession is always accompanied in these descriptions by the characteristic clinical signs of an abnormal state of the nervous system? Can we furnish an explanation, or indicate the cause, of this strange but none the less regular concomitance?

III. PRINCIPLES OF THE SOLUTION

To the question thus precisely put, mystical theology (falling back on dogmatic theology and on scholastic philosophy) provides important elements of the answer. We must now bring these elements together into some kind of synthesis. If, in so doing, our language seems at times a trifle technical, we trust the reader will excuse it.

Scholastic philosophy distinguishes two groups of faculties within the one indivisible human soul. One group belongs to the sensible order—imagination and sensibility; and the other to the intellectual—intelligence and will. When all is duly ordered in a human soul its activity is directed by the will, which commands both the imagination and the sensibility, according to the lights it receives from a reason informed by the truth. But reason, in its turn, under the normal conditions of its exercise here below, is only capable of attaining to the truth if the sense faculties provide it with a suitable aliment that they themselves have prepared. This interaction between the faculties affects also the will, whose decisions may be influenced, even very strongly, by the attractions brought to bear on it from the side of the sensibility. However, the hierarchy of the faculties remains, and the will *alone* sovereignly decides the *free* act, which it can carry out, postpone or omit as it chooses.

But—still following the teaching of scholastic philosophy—it is the above-mentioned spiritual soul that gives life to the body, animates or "informs" it. There are not two souls in man, one spiritual and the other corporeal, but one only. Now it is precisely by its lower powers, by the sensibility, that the immaterial soul puts out its hold on the body. In the one unique but composite being of the human individual, it is here that we find the point of junction. If we approach this indivisible point from the side of the spiritual soul, we shall call it the sensibility; if we approach it from the side of the life of the body, we shall present it as the vital movement proper to the nervous system. This very close union between the nervous system, which pertains to the body, and the sensibility, which is a faculty of the soul, permits the transmission of the commands of the will to the body and its movements. It is this union that is dissolved by death. It is this union that is weakened by mental disorders; for these are definable as disorders of the nervous system, carrying *ipso facto* a disorder of the same importance into the sensibility, and resulting at the limit in madness. Then the will finds all the machinery of command put out of action and no longer controls either the sensibility or the nervous system, which are both abandoned to their only two alternatives of dazed depression or of furious excitement.

Now it is precisely at this point of intersection and liaison between soul and body that theologians locate the action of the devil. He cannot, any more than other creatures, act directly on the intelligence or the will: that domain is strictly reserved to the human person himself and to God his Creator.[1] All that the devil can do is to influence the higher faculties indirectly, by provoking tendentious representations in the imagination, and disordered movements in the sensitive appetite, with corresponding perturbations in the nervous system, synchronized as it is with the sensibility. Thereby he hopes to deceive the intelligence, especially in its practical judgments, and still more especially to weigh in on the will and induce its consent to bad acts. As long as things stop there we have "temptation".

But—with God's permission, accorded for the greater supernatural good of souls, or to put no constraint on the freedom of their malice—things need not stop there. The devil can profit from a disorder introduced into the human composite by a mental malady. He can even provoke and amplify the functional disequilibrium, and take advantage of

---

[1] This doctrine is developed *ex professo* by St. Thomas, *Sum. Theol.*, i, q. 111, arts. 1 and 4, synthetised in I–II, q. 80, art. 2, and often recalled throughout the II Pars. (for example, in I–II, q. 9, art. 6). In mystical theology it is classic, see for example Schram, *Theol. mystica,* vol. 1, §208–25 and especially §208: *Quid daemon in possessis possit,* 5. The mystics claim to have direct experience of this impotence of the demon, see e.g. St. Teresa, *Life,* ch. xvii.

it to insinuate and install himself at the point of least resistance. There he gets control of the mechanism of command, mánipulates it at his pleasure, and so indirectly reduces to impotence both the intelligence and, above all, the will; which for their proper exercise require that the sensible data shall be correctly presented and that the means of transmission shall be in good working order. Such are the main lines of the theory of diabolic possession worked out by Catholic theology. Let us note that if death, and so also the ills that prepare it, came into the world, this was "by the envy of the devil" turned against our first parents (Wisd. ii. 24), a thing that justifies the title by which he was stigmatised by Jesus: "A murderer from the beginning" (John viii. 44). By fastening, in possession, on the precise point at which body and soul are knit together but can be disassociated, he maintains the line of operations that he chose from the start in order to wage his war against humanity.

If all this is correct, we shall have to infer with the theologians that all true diabolic possession is accompanied, in fact and by a quasi-necessity, by mental and nervous troubles produced or amplified by the demon, and yet having manifestations and symptoms which are practically and medically identical with those produced by neuroses. The psychiatrist, therefore, is free to study these symptoms, to describe these mental troubles, and to indicate their immediate causes. There he stands on his own ground. But if, in the name of his science, he pre-

tends to exclude *a priori*, and in all cases, any trans-
cendent cause of the anomalies in question, then he
trespasses beyond the bounds of his special com-
petence. Precisely by confining himself to his own
methods he automatically foregoes any inquiry of
this kind. Never will he find the devil at the term of
his purely medical analysis, any more than the sur-
geon will find the soul at the point of his scalpel,
or any more than the dog, seeing his master in anger,
can estimate the moral or immoral character of these
strange gesticulations: all that belongs to another
order. But the doctor who wants to remain a complete man, above all if he enjoys the light of the faith,
will never exclude *a priori*, and in some cases may
well suspect, the presence and action of some occult
power behind the malady. He will hand over its
investigation to the philosopher and the theologian,
allowing himself to be guided by their methods; and
he will have enough modesty to remember that where
his medical science, brought to bear on a woman
who cannot hold herself up straight, will see nothing
but a partial paralysis of eighteen years' standing,
the penetrating and infallible glance of Jesus dis-
cerned and asserted the presence of the devil putting
forth all his hatred against a daughter of Abraham.

With this, then, we return to the Gospel and to
its diabolical possessions. It is precisely to account
for it all that Catholic theologians have elaborated
the theory sketched above. It is the business of the
psychologists and the doctors to complete the sketch
by providing it with all the precise analyses and

formulae which the progress of modern science permits and requires. It is also for them to say whether it would not be very advantageous, for the medical profession and theologians alike, to drop the attitude of suspicious isolation in which they stand to each other, and to unite their efforts and methods with a view to obtaining a truly adequate interpretation of facts relating to several complementary branches of human knowledge—facts such as the diabolic possessions of the Gospel and their healing by Jesus.